Contents

ACKNOWLEDGEMENTS

This book could not have been prepared without the help of many people. I am particularly grateful to:

- the members of Her Majesty's Inspectorate, with whom I recently had the privilege of working.

- the staff of all the nurseries I have visited, for allowing me to observe their work and for numerous useful discussions.

- the friends and colleagues who have read and commented on successive drafts of the review.

- Dorothy Merritt for her patient and enthusiastic secretarial support.

- Judy, my wife, who created the harmonious atmosphere in which I was able to think and write.

Chapter I

Experiments in nursery education

Introduction

In Britain during the past decade we have witnessed a major upsurge of interest in the provision of educational facilities for children who have not yet attained the age of compulsory school attendance, (five-years-old). Increasingly parents have sought a place for their child in a nursery, eager that he should obtain the best possible start to his education. However places in nursery schools and classes are only available to a small proportion of three-and four-year-olds, (approximately 10 per cent of the one-and-a-half-million in the age-group, DES, 1974).

In the absence of State nursery provision many resourceful parents, local groups and charities have set up their own 'playgroups'. This form of voluntary provision has grown into a movement co-ordinated by the Pre-School Playgroups Association (PPA) which it is estimated now caters for 250,000 children (PPA, 1974). For many parents, other considerations besides the educational needs of their children have also influenced their demand for nursery facilities. Increasingly mothers have found it necessary and desirable to return to employment while their children are still quite young. These parents have sought a place for their child in one of the less than 500 local authority day-nurseries which offer day-care facilities (DHSS, 1974a).

Administrators and other professionals concerned with the education and welfare of the under-fives have long recognized the value of nursery experience as a transition between home and school, and the need also to provide day-care facilities in a modern urban industrial society. Recognition of the large unfulfilled demand for nursery education prompted the Plowden Committee to devote a chapter of their report on British primary education to recommendations for the large-scale expansion of nursery provision (Central Advisory Council for

Education, 1967, vol. 1, chap. 9). Subsequently these recommendations were substantially incorporated within a major statement of government policy contained in the White Paper of 1972 (DES, 1972). We are currently observing the efforts of local authorities to make nursery expansion a reality, despite the stifling effects of economic recession.

Finally researchers have played their own part in provoking and sustaining some of the current interest in the education of the under-fives. Research can provide information, assess current provision and evaluate innovations, and there is an abundant research literature which might be used to guide the direction of future developments in nursery provision. Barbara Tizard (1975) has provided a valuable comprehensive survey of the many recent and current British research projects which have examined issues relevant to the development of provision. The purpose of this book is to offer an extended account of only a small part of this research. The single issue which has generated the most controversy and the most strenuous research effort centres on the possiblity of using nursery education as a means of reducing educational and ultimately social inequalities between children. These research projects are most often referred to as experiments in 'compensatory education'.

The focus of such experiments is on a group of children who consistently appear to be of lower ability than is normal for their age and characteristically have difficulties coping with the demands of school. But the group is defined not by ability but by the economic and social circumstances of their families. These are the 'children of poverty', the 'socially disadvantaged', the 'culturally deprived'. These are some of the many terms which have been coined to express the one central idea that for these children school failure is not determined by any lack of inborn potential but by home circumstances which are deficient in the kind of experiences which would equip them for school-learning.

The philosophy of 'equality of opportunity' has guided much of our social and educational planning in recent years. Advocates of compensatory education argue that this philosophy cannot offer true equality to children who commence school already at a disadvantage compared with their peers. It merely provides them with the 'opportunity' to demonstrate their 'inequality'.

Education alone cannot redress this balance; to do so would demand that radical changes also be made in the economic and social circumstances of these children and their families. However our task here is to explore the role which education can play. Above all else, pre-school education has been singled out as the most promising strategy for improving the educational attainment of these children. It is argued that suitable nursery provision provided selectively for these children could 'compensate' for their adverse home circumstances and render them more equal with their peers when they commence compulsory schooling. This review will describe research designed to find what might be the most 'suitable' nursery provision.

The review arises out of recognition of a rift which often exists between researchers and those policy-makers, administrators and teachers at all levels, who might make use of and be guided by the findings of their research. The existence of the rift is evidenced by the misconceptions under which those not closely familiar with research reports may work.

By way of illustration, it is commonly believed that experiments in compensatory education have been conducted exclusively in the USA, and that they have failed. The Westinghouse evaluation of Headstart (Cicirelli *et al.*, 1969), is most frequently cited. The explanation for this 'failure' is often sought in the arguments for the 'high heritability' of intelligence which have been presented by Jensen (1969) and popularized by Eysenck (1971). Secondly, there is general mistrust of American research findings on the grounds that circumstances are different here and 'intercontinental' generalizations are invalid. What is often not appreciated is that there is a growing body of British research which can throw light on these issues in the context of local pre-school traditions.

In this review the design and results of various projects will be discussed with a view to the implications they may have for the development of pre-school education. As far as possible the review will illustrate the relevant issues by reference to research conducted in the British context, since it is the development of British education with which readers are most likely to be concerned. But before launching into the main account, it will be useful to mention briefly the American work, by way of introduction, since it has been extremely influential on British ideas and is the direct forerunner of much of the British research.

The American Headstart Programme

The most comprehensive account of American projects may be found in Little and Smith (1971); a briefer outline is contained in Halsey (1972). In 1964 President Johnson announced the 'War on Poverty' which included a major project for pre-school children funded through the Federal Office of Economic Opportunity. Initially in 1965 an eight-week summer programme was set up in pre-school centres throughout the country, locally administered by school boards, religous organizations, community action groups etc. The demand was so great that by 1967, 215,000 children were attending full-year centres, and a larger number attending summer courses. This has come to be known as the 'Headstart' programme. The project did not have a major built-in evaluation element, and it was only on completion of many of the schemes that an evaluation was sought by the Office of Economic Opportunity. A research project was set up jointly by the Westinghouse Learning Corporation and Ohio University to make a retrospective assessment of the benefits of the programme. The pessimistic findings expressed in the subsequent 'Westinghouse Report' (Cicirelli *et al.*, 1969) have been chiefly responsible for subsequent cutbacks in funds for pre-school programmes, and for this reason the evaluation is worth examining in a little detail. The scope of the evaluation was limited to answering the question:

'Does the cognitive and affective development of primary-grade school children who have had Headstart experience differ significantly from that of comparable children who have not had such experience?'

(Cicirelli *et al.*, 1969 vol. 1 p. 33.)

Since the Headstart programmes had already been in operation for some years, and the time allotted for the study was short, it was not possible to adopt accepted experimental procedures of selecting a group of Headstart and a group of control (non-Headstart) children and comparing their abilities before and after the programme.

Instead a group of children were identified who had already experienced Headstart and were now in first, second or third grade (i.e. six- seven- or eight-year-olds). Their abilities were assessed, and compared with those of a comparison group matched on all relevant criteria, (e.g. age, ethnic group, sex, socioeconomic status, location of residence and school experience), except the crucial one, experience of a Headstart programme.

A national sample of 4,000 children was assessed on measures of verbal ability, attainment, attitude to school etc. Despite exhaustive statistical treatment of the data, the number of measures on which there were significant differences was extremely small, and some of these even favoured the comparison groups rather than those who had experienced Headstart.

So great was the egalitarian fervour and financial investment behind Headstart, that the long list of 'non-significances' published by the Westinghouse Corporation caused a sharp reaction, and was followed by series of fierce debates about the correct interpretation of the findings, and their educational and policy implications. The conclusions have been dissected from all angles as each specialist tries to use the results to justify and expound on his particular position. (See for example: Campbell and Erlebacher 1970; Jensen 1969 and Jencks *et al.*, 1973).

Three main types of explanation for the failure of Headstart may be singled out. There are those who blame the failure principally on the inadequacy and poor quality of the programmes; others have paid greatest attention to inadequacies in the evaluation of the programmes; but the explanation which has received the most popular attention points to the inadequacies of the environmentalist theory of individual differences in child learning on which compensatory programmes are based.

This is not the place to discuss these interpretations. It is perhaps most important to recognize that as an attempt to show that compensatory education is possible, Headstart is not a good example. It was not a model programme and the evaluation included children who had attended both 'good' and 'bad' pre-school centres. Much more valuable evidence may be obtained from the smaller-scale more controlled research projects which have been conducted in the USA over a number of years. Accounts of some of these studies may be found in Stanley (1972, 1973); their results have also been summarized by Bronfennbrenner (1972). Some will be mentioned in the context of the British projects to which we now turn.

Background to the British projects

The British projects are fewer in number and smaller in scale of operation than the American. The immediate impetus of much of the research was the Plowden Committee's recommendation that if true educational equality was to be achieved, ensuring equality of opportunity would not be sufficient (Central Advisory Council for Education 1967, vol. 1, Chap. 5). What was required was positive discrimination to provide the very best educational experiences for disadvantaged children. The Plowden Committee was particularly concerned about the evidence of 'cumulative deprivation'; that social disadvantage tends to be concentrated in particular areas, and that far from alleviating the situation, the schools in these areas tend to be of lower standard, and consequently reinforce children's disadvantage.

'We ask for "positive discrimination" in favour of such schools and children in them, going well beyond an attempt to equalise resources. Schools in deprived areas should be given priority in many respects. The first step must be to raise the schools with low standards to the national average; the second, quite deliberately to make them better'.

(Central Advisory Council for Education 1967, vol. 1, para. 151).

Accordingly the Plowden Committee recommended the designation of 'Educational Priority Areas' (EPAs) which were to be provided with extra resources for education. Most of the positive discrimination measures were to be directed to primary schools. For example, a higher quota of teachers was to be allowed and extra allowances paid to them; and old buildings were to be improved. However one of the measures was directly concerned with the provision of nursery education in priority areas.

The Plowden Committee also argued that a research project should be set up to evaluate the various measures taken (Central Advisory Council for Education, 1967, vol. 1, para: 170). A number of action-research projects developed either directly or indirectly out of this proposal. Most attention has been focused on the research which was jointly sponsored by the Department of Education and Science and a research body, the Social Science Research Council, under the overall direction of A.H. Halsey. £175,000 was allocated for a three-year programme (1968/9—1971/2) in four areas of England: West Riding, Birmingham, Deptford and Liverpool. An additional programme was also begun in Dundee. Each group was locally based with its own research staff. The project has come to be known as 'the EPA experiment'. The reports of this research will be one of the principal sources for this review (Halsey, 1972; Payne, 1974; Barnes, 1975; Smith, 1975; Morrison *et al.*, 1974; Midwinter, 1972). The review will be selective; the research covered primary as well as pre-school education, although it is only the latter that will be described here. Another major project which arose out of Plowden was the Schools Council project directed by Chazan. However with one exception (Chazan, Laing and Jackson, 1971) this research was almost entirely focused on the infant schools and will not be discussed here. The reader is referred to the following reports, (Chazan, 1973; and forthcoming). Other compensatory work in the infant school is reported in Gahagan and Gahagan (1970).

The other main source of British research for the review is the NFER's own 'Pre-School Project' which commenced in 1968 under the direction of H.L. Williams. This project was concerned solely with evaluating pre-school education for disadvantaged children (Williams, 1973; and Woodhead, 1976).

The projects described here are often referred to as 'action-research' because they are experiments which also involve introducing change in a social and educational situation. Considerable difficulties have been encountered in reconciling 'action' with 'research'. Effective action requires flexibility, sensitivity to the changing demands of a situation, and continuous modifications in strategy. This contrasts with the needs of conventional research for controlled intervention to make evaluation and interpretation of results possible. Evidence of such difficulties are described throughout the research reports (and particularly Halsey,

1972, chap. 3). Suffice it to note here that compromise was sought for and usually achieved.

The concept of disadvantage

The diverse strategies described here are united by their aim to improve the educational experiences of disadvantaged children. There is no precise definition of 'disadvantage'. The concept arises out of the evidence of longitudinal studies which have identified the relationship between failure at school and children's home circumstances, for example Douglas (1964); Davie, Butler and Goldstein (1972). For a brief account see Wedge and Prosser (1973). Such studies have found that low attainment is associated with social background characteristics which describe very well the home circumstances of many children living in urban poverty: low social class, limited parent education, large family, overcrowding, poor quality housing etc. Considerable caution should be observed in drawing conclusions from these studies. The concept of disadvantage which they generate is essentially a statistical construction which describes the association between home circumstances and attainments for a large group. Strictly speaking we should not extrapolate from these studies into such statements as 'the needs of the disadvantaged child are. . . . . . etc.'. The same rule applies to the projects described here. Research generally deals in overall patterns and trends for large groups of children. It should not be assumed that conclusions drawn for a group will apply to any one individual child.

All of the research work described in this book has this common starting point, the evidence of school failure related to the social circumstances of groups of children. But the precise explanation of failure and prescription for action differ greatly. The variety of approach may be illustrated by contrasting two extreme models.

The dominant interpretation of failure has placed the emphasis on the inadequacies of a child's home; the origin of the child's difficulites at school and his failure to match up to recognized criteria of attainment lie in the deficiencies of his early educational experiences. Accordingly the model predicts that the way to improve the child's performance is to introduce an early education programme which compensates for these deficiencies. This model is most often associated with the policy of 'positive discrimination'. It argues that a superficial equality of access to education does not take into account that some children are at a disadvantage before they start. Consequently the road to true equality is through providing extra education for the disadvantaged groups. Many of the recommendations of the Plowden report are argued in these terms.

An alternative model rejects both this explanation for failure and this prescription for equality. The central point is neatly expressed by

Basil Bernstein:

> 'The concept, "compensatory education", serves to direct attention away from the internal organisation and the educational context of the school, and focus our attention on the families and children. "Compensatory education" implies that something is lacking in the family, and so in the child. As a result, the children are unable to benefit from schools.'
>
> (Bernstein, 1970)

The alternative interpretation is that the deficiencies lie in the school, which does not provide an appropriate environment for the children, by virtue of its failure to adopt teaching methods and educational goals which are relevant to the children's experience. Adopting a sociological perspective, this model views the culture of both the working class and middle class home as equally valid and having a contribution to make in education; neither is deficient, but they are different. The middle class child succeeds at school only because the educational experiences and values of the school accord with those of his home. The "equality" sought by advocates of compensatory education is all too often a middle class uniformity. The alternative model argues that the greatest change must be in the schools and teachers who must develop goals and methods which appeal to the children's experiences and are sensitive to the life circumstances of their families.

These are extremes and it would be wrong to identify any particular research project with either approach. The perspectives underlying the research cover all shades of opinion within these extremes. Of course the author has his own perspective on the educational implications of social disadvantage which will affect the interpretation of research reported. At risk of anticipating the conclusions of this review it may be useful to summarize this position at the outset.

The approach which seeks to 'compensate' for the 'deficient' home background of 'socially' disadvantaged children places too high expectations on the school as an agency of social change. Premature, over-ambitious claims were made for the Headstart programme in the USA which could not be substantiated by research results. We should not make the same mistake in Britain. More modest expectations for early education programmes which have some chance of being achieved in practice are preferable. Equally, an approach which rejects the relevance of conventional educational goals and methods for certain groups of children is in danger of undermining the teacher's own confidence in his competence and, far from counteracting socially divisive educational methods, may unwittingly perpetuate them.

The approach taken here will be a pragmatic one, which uses 'disadvantage' to characterize all those individuals, groups, and communities, who are for one reason or another, either through the circumstances of the homes or shortcomings of the school, failing to profit from the educational experiences made available to them. Inevitably, since we have greater direct control over the environment of the school than we have over the home, the emphasis will be on ways in which the school can be modified to provide a better service for these groups.

Three particular aspects of pre-school education will be considered and evaluated in this review. British research has paid greatest attention to the development and evaluation of pre-school curricula for disadvantaged children. Accordingly, this is the first topic of the review and takes up the greater part of its length (Chapters 2, 3, 4 and 5). A great deal of interest, but far less British research has been invested in the second topic: the value of working with the parents of pre-school children, (described in Chapter 6). Finally the topic which most urgently requires action and research has received the least attention to date. Development and evaluation of pre-school curricula presuppose that disadvantaged pre-school children currently benefit from an educational experience. Chapter 7 describes the research which is available on the provision of nursery education for these children.

Chapter II

Nursery traditions and research objectives

In this, and succeeding chapters, we shall be describing the attempts of the EPA and NFER research teams to design, develop and evaluate nursery programmes especially intended for pre-school children from disadvantaged home circumstances. These projects were born of a marriage between educational research methods and nursery education practices. The research workers included educationists, psychologists and sociologists, many of whom had practical experience in pre-school and primary education, but whose main current concern was in the development and evaluation of educational programmes for young children. The practitioners included LEA administrators and advisers, nursery heads, teachers and assistants who were daily providing a nursery education service on limited resources. In most cases the researchers courted the practitioners, viewing the captive group of pre-school children as a suitable sample for whom to develop and evaluate special nursery programmes.

At first sight the two partners might appear to have been most well-matched. They were united by a common conviction that children's early experiences are crucial to their subsequent development and that nursery education has an important role to play in enriching the experiences of children from disadvantaged home circumstances.

The compensatory tradition in nursery education

Nursery education has a long tradition of 'compensating' for the home, although that particular expression has only been used relatively recently. The pioneers in this respect were the McMillan sisters who were responsible for running a nursery for the slum children of Deptford during the second decade of the century. The 'nursery school' developed directly out of their early campaigns to encourage the setting up of school clinics. The sisters soon recognized the limitations of a medical service which cured children's ailments but did not prevent them recurring because no effort was made to alter the circumstances in which they lived. The 'open air nursery school' was designed to provide the healthy environment which was lacking in the children's home experience. Accordingly, the particular emphasis of the nursery regime was on improving the health of the children as well as increasing their awareness and understanding of their environment.

The idealism with which the sisters approached this task is illustrated by this extract from Margaret McMillan's book, first published in 1919, in which she described the beneficial effects of nursery school experience:

> 'After luncheon and in the afternoon the gate of the nursery opens, and a troop of lovely children file out and pass, a river of beauty and grace, up the dim alley, and across the sordid square flanked by public houses. Women stop in their hurried errands; men coming to and fro, or standing idle by the street corner, turn softened eyes on this line of nurtured children. Are they really children of this neighbourhood? Did any one of these ever run in the gutter, or linger, shockheaded, near a dirty closehead? We need not ask such questions now. Already the past is far away. These children come to school every morning clean and fair. If many still take the school bath it is because they love it, many do not need it any more. And how do they differ from the well-groomed nurslings of Hyde Park or of Mayfair? Certainly they should not, and we believe will not differ from them through any lower standard of purity or nurture.
>
> Thus far we have won already in the Nursery School.'
>
> (McMillan, 1930, pp. 9—10)

The arguments for providing nursery education especially for disadvantaged children have been stated and re-stated in all the major documents on early education during this century. Tessa Blackstone (1971) has documented the development of this tradition from the first legislation which made financial support for nursery schools possible, namely the Education Act of 1918. The 1908 report of a Consultative Committee set up by the Board of Education serves as an illustration of early thinking.

The Committee considered that the most appropriate place for children under five was in the home, and that the purpose of establishing nursery schools should be to cater for children whose home circumstances were unsatisfactory. The Committee recognized the importance of local determination of the needs of an area, and advocated that most of the provision should be concentrated in the urban areas.

Some shifts of emphasis are discernible in more recent reports which have discussed nursery education, notably Hadow (1933) and Plowden (Central Advisory Council for Education, 1967); but the general sentiment remains much the same.

Increasingly the general desirability of nursery education for all children has been recognized. Although the emphasis on the special needs of 'disadvantaged' children remains the same, the precise character of their needs has changed. The arguments of the early campaigners, especially the McMillan Sisters, were directed towards the value of nursery schooling in promoting the health and physical welfare of children living in urban poverty. The precise focus for 'compensatory' work has now shifted to reflect the changing character of urban poverty. Following the general improvement of health education and medical and welfare facilities, attention has increasingly been directed towards other aspects of children's home circumstances which might prove detrimental to their development. For example, nursery practitioners have recognized an important role for the nursery in providing emotional security for children from broken homes, social experiences for isolated or only—children, and opportunities for cognitive development for children whose home circumstances only permit restricted play experiences with limited materials, where parents are unable or unwilling actively to promote their children's understanding of experiences and use of language to communicate them.

At the time when the research projects were being planned, nursery provision seemed an ideal site for introducing a special programme to disadvantaged children. Arguably nursery schools and classes have been practising compensatory education for 50 years. Since they are available only to a minority of children and are concentrated in the deprived areas, they are designed in a very real sense to be bases for positive discrimination, the heart of the compensatory education philosophy.

Not surprisingly then, nursery schools and classes provided the context for many of the experiments we shall describe. The NFER project worked exclusively in nursery schools, while the EPA teams mostly worked in nursery classes attached to primary schools. In some cases the EPA teams also used playgroups. Although the majority of playgroups have not been designed on the same philosophy of compensatory education, those used by the EPA teams were amongst the considerable number which have been set up by a local social services department or voluntary body especially to serve children from disadvantaged homes.

However compatible the marriage between the goals of the research and the aims underlying nursery practices might at first have seemed, closer examination reveals that quite fundamental divisions existed which were to affect the character of the research projects as well as their success. The division did not stem from the unacceptability of the methods which the researchers wished to employ, their use of experimental and control groups, and administration of standardized tests to such young children. The justification for these techniques required explanation, of course, but this was not to prove a major obstacle. The question of which type of educational programme the researchers should develop and evaluate was to prove a much more contentious issue. Disagreement centred on different attitudes to the needs of young disadvantaged children and the educational methods which were most appropriate.

In simplest terms these differences may be stated as follows. The overall goal of the researchers was to evaluate the success of a nursery programme in overcoming the lack of competence of many young disadvantaged children in the intellectual and language skills which are important for coping with the demands of later schooling. Accordingly, their view of the role of nursery education emphasized the unique opportunity it provides to ensure that all children have acquired basic competence before they begin compulsory schooling. They argued that if intensive instructional methods are used, the nursery has the potential to offset any inadequacies of the home and render children more equal as they enter primary school at five years old.

Although the aim of improving language and intellectual skills would be acknowledged by nursery practitioners, this is set within a much broader group of aims for nursery education. Generally speaking the function of nursery education has not been to prepare children for school, and the direct instructional methods normally associated with a later stage of education have generally been rejected as inappropriate for children of nursery age.

It is, of course, a grave oversimplification to state these two extremes of opinion, identifying one with the researchers and the other with the teachers. All 'shades of opinion are apparent in both groups. Nevertheless the general trend was certainly in this direction, and it will be worth exploring in a little more detail the educational philosophy and traditions of nursery education, as a background to appreciating the various approaches taken by the researchers.

The aims and methods of nursery education

By way of illustration we may turn to the writings of two of the most influential British nursery educationists. In discussing the regime most suited to the child of nursery age, great emphasis has been placed on the importance of providing the child with the freedom to explore experiences and learn through self-chosen activities. For example Susan Isaacs concluded her discussion, first published in 1929, as follows:

'For the moment perhaps enough has been said to show how large a value children's play has for all sides of their growth. How great an ally the thoughtful parent can find it! And how fatal to go against this great stream of healthy and active impulse in our children! That "restlessness" and inability to sit still; that "mischievousness" and eternal "Why?"; that indifference to soiled hands and torn clothes for the sake of running and climbing and digging and exploring — these are not unfortunate and accidental ways of childhood which are to be shed as soon as we can get rid of them. They are the glory of the human child, his human heritage. They are at once the representatives in him of human adventurousness and hard-won wisdom, and the means by which he in his turn will lay hold of knowledge and skill, and add to them.'

(Isaacs, 1968).

This is clearly a reaction against traditional methods of childrearing which might have constrained the child to behave as a young adult and 'only speak when he's spoken to'. Dorothy Gardner neatly summarized the three conditions under which she believed children's learning may be best promoted.

Firstly, she argued, the nursery must provide an environment which contains objects to stimulate the children's curiosity. Secondly, children must be allowed the freedom to learn by direct experience, and at their own pace. Finally, participation by the adult in children's play is regarded as most important:

'She sometimes participates in their play, when to do so will give them helpful ideas, makes useful suggestions and responds to those made by the children. She gives incidental information when interest is aroused and puts the children in the way of gaining fresh knowledge and experience. She is quick to recognise a child's problem and help him to solve it, and to realise when a question, comment or demonstration from her will lead the children on to fresh achievements and can carry their interests into wider fields.'

(Gardner, 1956).

The currency of this philosophy is apparent from the more recent publications by Marianne Parry and Hilda Archer (1974, 1975) and Lesley Webb (1975).

A different source of information on the aims and methods of nursery education comes from the survey of teachers' attitudes by Philip Taylor *et al* (1972). The 578 teachers in Taylor's sample recognized the particular value of nursery experience for disadvantaged children. This is indicated by the finding that 'children from deprived homes' and 'children from Educational Priority Areas' are mentioned most often as groups for whom nursery education is essential, by over 85 per cent of the sample. However, the teachers' answers to the other questions suggest that they do not give highest priority to the attainment of specific educational objectives for these children. In terms of overall priorities, intellectual aims take second place to social aims. And when these broad aims are analysed in terms of specific objectives it is clear that by 'intellectual' the teachers are thinking of very general abilities, e.g. 'help child reason', 'take initiative in problem solving', placing specific intellectual objectives, e.g. 'classify', 'measure, count, match sets', at the very bottom of the list.

These priorities are quite predictable from a knowledge of the traditions underlying the nursery school philosophy. The first nursery schools were not set up as preparation grounds for primary schools, and nursery staffs have never taken the demands of later education as the main source of their aims; on the contrary. We have already referred to the recommendations of the 1908 Consultative Committee to set up nursery schools especially for children from unsatisfactory homes. Far from being intended to prepare children for the infant school education of the day, these nurseries were designed to offer an alternative to the common practice of admitting children under five to the 'babies classes' of infant schools. Blackstone (1971) quotes Board of Education statistics which show that the proportion of three- to five-year-olds on school registers had increased from 24 per cent in 1870—1 to 43 per cent in 1900—1. The arguments against this trend were most forcefully expressed in a Report by Woman Inspectors of the Board of Education in 1905, summarized as follows:

'. . . the mechanical teaching in many infant schools seems to dull rather than awaken the little power of imagination and independent observation which these children possess.'

(quoted in Blackstone, 1971).

The report argued that since the formal instruction of the infant school is likely to be detrimental to these children, then they would be better off staying at home with their mothers. Subsequently, there was a sharp decline in the numbers of children in the babies' classes.

The recommendation of the 1908 Committee that the nursery schools for disadvantaged children should be *separate* from the infant schools is of considerable significance, and might be seen as a symbol that the educators of young children were turning their backs on the infant school as a model for their work. The traditional opposition to formal instruction in nursery education has survived to this day.

Accordingly, while nursery schools and classes have traditionally provided a programme for disadvantaged children, it is not primarily determined by a conception of what the child might need for later school success. The model adopted by British nursery education may be identified most closely with a belief that the child's development should be allowed to follow a 'natural' course. This belief was central to the European kindergarten movement associated with Friedrich Froebel (Lilley, 1967). The philosophy was extremely influential on the development of British nursery education in the early part of the century and remains prevalent to this day (Lawrence, 1952).

The research background

The general view of the researchers contrasted strongly with this picture of 'natural' development, and emphasized that the course of a child's development is largely determined by the influences of home and school, and may be modified through suitable intervention at an early age. Their starting point was the evidence of inequalities in educational attainment between disadvantaged and more advantaged children which are apparent early in their school life and which become more marked as the years pass. Current theory argues that the origins of these inequalities lie in the children's home experiences, particularly the differences in use of language between the groups, adapted to their social circumstances and life-style. The best known formulation of this theory has been presented by Basil Bernstein. He distinguishes a 'restricted' from an 'elaborated' code or form of language.

> 'In the case of an elaborated code, such a code points to the possibilities which inhere in a complex hierarchy for the organisation and expression of inner experience. This is much less the case where experience is regulated by a restricted code, for this code orients its speakers to a less complex conceptual hierarchy and so to a lower order of causality.'
>
> (Bernstein 1971a, p. 151).

Bernstein argues that elaborated-code users are better prepared for the demands of education which requires making meanings explicit. The research team working with Bernstein have identified in some detail the linguistic features of the two codes, and have provided evidence that middle class speakers are more competent in use of elaborated code than working class speakers (Bernstein 1971b, 1973). This theory has been the subject of considerable discussion and contradictory evidence, some of which will be discussed in a later chapter. But the general proposition was accepted by most of the researchers working on the projects we are discussing. For them the implication was clear. An important role for any early education programme must be to encourage proficiency of children in both the structural and functional possibilities of language. The programme currently being offered in many nursery schools and classes did not seem likely to fulfil this requirement. Although the researchers were eager to avoid interfering unduly in children's self-initiated play activities, it became apparent that injection into the programme of a more structured, intensive language-teaching element was required if nurseries were to prepare children better for the demands of later education.

This argument against the traditional nursery programme has been most emphatically stated by Bereiter and Englemann (1966), in the context of a programme they established in the USA. They criticize the inappropriateness of the goals and methods of the traditional pre-school programme to the problems of the disadvantaged. They cite studies which show these children to be retarded on measures of intelligence, by up to one year at the age of three to five years. If these children are to 'catch-up' with their more advantaged peers, then, Bereiter and Englemann argue, they must learn at a faster rate. The traditional nursery does not provide the context in which such rapid rates of development are possible; the emphasis on social and emotional development through free play admirably complements the structured 'academic' home of the middle class child, but does not suit the needs of disadvantaged children. If the nursery is to be designed to complement the home of the disadvantaged child it must offer a more structured 'academic' programme; the non-academic objectives must be relegated to second place.

By now it will be clear that for the researchers, the task of introducing a compensatory programme for pre-school children was by no means a simple matter. It did not simply involve providing selected disadvantaged children with nursery experience enriched with a few extra activities thought appropriate to their needs. In many cases it also involved introducing educational objectives and a style of teaching quite alien to that normally practised in nursery education.

The importance of this basis conflict between the methods of compensatory programmes and the tradition of nursery education is not to be underestimated. It was to colour the success of all the programmes. Most importantly the conflict was recognized to a different extent by different project teams, and each provided a different resolution to the problem. These various resolutions are the subject of the next chapter.

Chapter III

Design of intervention programmes in the nursery

The researchers' task was to select and evaluate a programme designed to improve the language and general intellectual abilities of nursery age children. The most likely candidate was the conventional programme found in most nursery schools, classes and playgroups, but this was soon recognized to be unsuitable. Most evaluation studies have come to the conclusion that nursery attendance does not have a marked effect on children's performance on measures of general ability. For a discussion of these studies see Swift (1964), Sjolund (1973), Webb (1974) and Thompson (1975). This finding is not at all surprising when considered in the light of the discussion of the previous chapter. To improve children's intellectual abilities has never been the principal objective of nursery education. Consequently, the problem for the researchers became how to introduce a specific language and cognitive programme which could justifiably be evaluated in these terms.

One resolution would have been for the researchers to set up special nursery centres with their own trained staff to provide a nursery programme designed by the researchers and prescribed by the conclusions from research. This has been possible for some of the American research centres. But limitations of time and money, as well as in some cases the lack of practical educational expertise meant that most of the projects which we are discussing were committed from an early stage to working within already existing pre-school centres, either nursery schools, nursery classes or playgroups. Since the staffs of these centres were to be actively involved in teaching the programme it was essential for the researchers to compromise some of their more ambitious aims to the day-to-day realities of the nursery programme. For some the solution was to develop a programme working from within the normal nursery tradition and integrated within the nursery day. We shall come to these later.

But for the most part, the resources of the research teams did not permit a lengthy development phase, they were forced to select an already existing programme and fit it into the nursery day as well as possible. In practice this usually meant the nursery day was divided between normal activities and the special programme.

No British project ever went to the extremes advocated by Bereiter and Engelmann (1966). The formal features of their approach, which included drill-learning, were alien to the theoretical background of the researchers, who generally emphasized the importance of meaningful learning. It was also a 'total' programme which could only have been introduced if the research team had set up their own pre-school centres. The programme selected was most likely to be American, where most work had been completed, but it had to fit in readily with the British nursery routine.

I. The Peabody Language Development Kit (PLDK)

The Peabody Language Development Kit was an obvious choice, since it required only 20 minutes per day during which a small group of children were withdrawn from normal activities. Most nurseries possessed a staff room, a quiet area, (or even a quiet corridor in some cases) where the programme could be administered. Teachers who might not have tolerated a more extensive programme, viewing it as an intrusion on the children's free play, were prepared to concede that 20 minutes of more structured activities would probably not be harmful, and might even be beneficial for some of the children. Another consideration was the amount of staff time taken up by the programme. Although the use of nursery assistants means that nurseries are more generously staffed than primary classes, teachers would have resented being forced to pay exclusive attention to one group of children and neglect the rest of the group for more than a short period of the day.

In view of its suitability to the nursery context, it is not surprising that, of all the programmes discussed here, the Peabody Kit has been most extensively introduced and evaluated by the EPA and NFER research teams. Level P is one of a series of programmes of language and cognitive training which have been developed by Dunn, Horton and Smith (1968). The series covers the age-range three to ten years; level P has been designed specifically for children with mental ages of approximately three to five years. The Kit is designed as a series of 180 short lessons or units of approximately 20 minutes. Each 20 minute session is conducted by an adult with a small group of children withdrawn from the main class. The series is carefully designed so that later activities build on and extend what is learned in early sessions. The first units introduce a small core vocabulary of common words. Later units use this vocabulary as a basis for learning syntactical patterns; finally the use of language in various cognitive skills is practised. Although the organization may seem formal, presentation to the children is informal and emphasizes meaningfulness of activities. The whole series is hinged around the exploits of three puppet characters — P. Mooney, Elbert the Elephant and a Goose. A number of teaching materials have been designed to suit the interests of children of this age, including P. Mooney's 'Magic Stick', with an illuminated nose, the P. Mooney Bag which may be used for remembering-games, records of songs and stories, dolls and sets of clothes, a xylophone, geometric shapes and numerous sets of picture cards, portraying familiar themes in children's daily life.

The manual contains precise directions on the way to introduce each part of each lesson. Such detailed instructions are clearly intended to guide the teacher with limited nursery experience. The authors make clear that the activities may be adapted to suit their own inclinations. By the way of illustration here is a summary of a typical daily lesson from the beginning of the programme on the theme of 'parts of the body'.

Part A

1. *Story Time*: a recorded story is played, which introduces parts of the body accompanied by pictures.
2. *Conversation Time*: the pictures are shown again and the children invited to reconstruct the story.

Part B

3. *Looking — Critical Thinking Time*: Pictures are shown with body parts missing, individual children are asked to identify the missing parts.
4. *Activity Time*: The teacher makes a statement, e.g. 'I clap my hands', and the children perform the appropriate activity.

The lessons later in the programme follow a similar format, but the activities require more complex verbal processes. For example, the following lesson is on the theme of 'animals'.

Part A

1. *Classification Time*: 33 animal cards are placed in front of the children, who are asked to select an animal and make a sentence which identifies it and says whether or not it is a farm animal.
2. *Sentence Building Time*: The group are asked to make a sentence identifying each of the animals in turn. The xylophone is used to provide a simple tune to accompany each sentence.

Part B

3. *Looking — Matching Time*: A poster is displayed showing animals on the farm. Each child is asked to choose an animal and to make up a sentence about the animal from the picture cards.
4. *Listening — Activity Time*: A variation of the song *The Farmer in the Dell* is used to identify pairs of animals.

Each lesson is divided into Parts A and B, each part to last 20 minutes. Ideally, it is intended that one part be introduced in the morning and the other in the afternoon. In the case of most of the British projects this was not possible, as the children were usually only part-time attenders at the nursery. If the programme is administered precisely according to the manual, the 180 lessons are designed to provide activities for one year.

One of the attractions of the Kit to the British researchers was that it was completely self-contained, including all the materials required to illustrate the lessons. This not only made the introduction to pre-school centres with limited or varying equipment easier. It was appealing to researchers because of the control that it exerted over the experiences of the children, which made evaluation considerably easier.

Undoubtedly of additional appeal was that the Kit has been devised on a research base, there was a clear rationale for the design of the Kit and the theoretical framework was one with which researchers were in general sympathy. The manual cites the work of Luria (1961) and Vygotsky (1962) who have been so influential on cognitive psychology through their emphasis on the critical role of language not only in communication, but also as a regulator of action and an instrument of thought, 'inner-speech'. The Kit is based on a model of language processes developed by Osgood (1957). Although this particular model has largely been superceded by the major advances in psycholinguistics (summarized by Slobin (1971), following on from the work of Chomsky (1965), in structural linguistics (summarized by Greene 1972), it nevertheless provides a useful reference point from which to devise activities.

The Kit also has the attraction of having been devised for use with children who are retarded either intellectually, or because of their disadvantaged home circumstances. The authors illustrate American research which highlights the apparent deficiencies of disadvantaged children in use of oral language, and the Kit is designed accordingly to place emphasis on these skills.

The PLDK was introduced into nurseries by NFER's 'Pre-School Project' and the EPA 'National Pre-School Experiment' in three of the

Educational Priority Areas — Birmingham, Liverpool and the West Riding. In Deptford and Dundee the reluctance of teachers to use the PLDK caused the teams to develop their own pre-school programmes which will be described in a later section (pp. 34—35).

Despite the care with which PLDK was selected, many of the features which made it attractive to researchers proved to be major stumbling blocks when the programme was introduced into the nurseries. Helen Quigley, a member of the research team at NFER, was responsible for assessing the reactions of teachers and assistants using the programme in the EPA and NFER nurseries (Quigley, 1971; Woodhead, 1976).

The nursery teachers were divided between those who were openly hostile to the aims and methods of the Kit and those who had greater sympathy for the approach. All the teachers had some reservations about the Kit and these are predictable from knowledge of their training and philosophy. Concern was expressed about whether it was right to interrupt the children's play with structured activities, especially since many of the staff believed that all the educational experiences comprising the Kit could be found in any good nursery. However, none of them doubted that the children enjoyed the sessions.

In general, the nursery assistants viewed the programme much more favourably. They found it offered a challenge to them, and the guidance of the detailed manual useful. As one of the nursery assistants involved in the NFER project remarked: 'I came out thinking I had got into a rut and generally tried to smarten up what I did' (Woodhead, 1976, Chap. III).

It seems probable that the nursery assistants were more receptive to the methods of the Kit because they lacked the same depth of training in an alternative philosophy of education. Quigley remarks that many of the fears of the teachers could have been allayed if the rationale of the Kit had been better explained. In particular, those teachers who had been worried about teaching specific grammatical structures and vocabulary had failed to recognize their purpose as the foundation for their use in later activities. They had failed to view the 180 lessons as a coherent sequence of learning activities.

Undoubtedly many of the other criticisms which Quigley reports were entirely justified. These stemmed from the inappropriateness of transferring a programme designed for use in ill-equipped nursery centres, by untrained staff with American disadvantaged children to British children in well-equipped nursery schools staffed by trained teachers.

The inclusion of plastic fruit to illustrate some of the lessons caused protest from some of the teachers; indeed as the feature of the Kit which is most striking from a first glance, the plastic fruit has been the trigger for many hostile reactions. The preference for real over plastic fruit is entirely understandable; nevertheless the reason for their inclusion in the Kit is the not unreasonable assumption that real fruit may not always be available to the teachers, and that the 'teachers' for whom the Kit was originally intended may not have had sufficient resourcefulness to organize acquisition of these or similar materials.

The essence of the programme is the sequence of 180 activities; the materials comprising the Kit are in many ways superfluous, provided the teacher can improvise from the resources of the nursery. Similarly the detailed instructions in the manual which some teachers felt was an insult to their skill as experienced teachers, have been prepared by the authors to give guidance to the least experienced teacher likely to use the programme, and were not intended to be followed 'parrot-fashion'.

Clearly there were many ways in which PLDK could have benefited from anglicization before being evaluated in British nurseries. Unfortunately the resources of the EPA teams did not permit them to make any extensive revision. The teams hoped that children would be sufficiently familiar with American idioms through TV that this would not detract from the general appropriateness of the programme.

The research-team at NFER were fortunate in having a slightly longer period alloted for pilot work. They were able to devote one year to trying out the Kit with a group of children in one of the nursery schools, making a preliminary evaluation of its effectiveness and using this and other information as the basis for adapting the Kit, reducing the significance of some of the features which had provoked such hostile reactions from some teachers, and rendering it much more suitable for use in British nursery schools.

In particular, activities to develop vocabulary and grammar which English children already possessed on entry to the programme were removed and more relevant activities introduced, especially activities designed to teach mathematical concepts. This aspect of the revision was greatly assisted by a small survey which was conducted of nursery children's knowledge of the vocabulary and grammar assumed by the kit or taught within it, and the vocabulary which is assumed by familiar reading schemes. Many of the most blatant Americanisms were removed and replaced by English equivalents, and the precise details of activities replaced by more general guidance to teachers on the use of the programme and the sequencing of activities. Further details of the revision are described in Chapter III of the NFER report (Woodhead, 1976). The revised manual has subsequently been published (Quigley & Hudson, 1974).

II. Alternative language programmes

All of the alternative language programmes we shall discuss arose out of a similar feeling of dissatisfaction with the structured American character of the PLDK and a desire to develop a pre-school programme which would be relevant to the needs of the children and the context of the nursery school.

(i) *Individual Language Programme — (West Riding EPA)*

This is particularly true of the West Riding Project, who were very soon aware that the needs of their children might differ considerably from the urban-deprived child. Consequently, although they introduced and evaluated the Peabody Kit in some nurseries, they also chose to develop their own in others. Design of a relevant pre-school programme seemed to require closer identification of the implications of particular social circumstances on children's educational experiences.

It became apparent quickly that two traditional goals of pre-school education need not be embodied in any provision for these children, namely physical and social development. In this stable community the young children did not lack experience of playing with peers, peer groups seemed to take an important place in the children's experience from a very early age. There was plenty of evidence of physical skill and agility amongst these children playing together.

Accordingly the pre-school programme concentrated on aspects of the child's development which their pre-school experiences at home and with peers had not fostered. In particular the cramped conditions in many of the homes did not allow for creative work and familiarity with handling pencils, paint brushes etc. Similarly knowledge of the language to accompany these activities was lacking. And because many of the children's experiences were of vigorous play outside, they had little experience of quieter activities requiring extended concentration.

Having established the areas of development on which the programme would focus, the team faced the problem of determining a method which would offer more direction and intense teacher-child interaction than a traditional programme, but would not be at the expense of inhibiting the spontaneity of the child and denying his interests. They wanted to avoid the superficial learning which may result from teaching by drill.

Design of the programme was strongly influenced by the work in New York by Marion Blank (Blank and Solomon, 1969; Blank 1973). Dr. Blank has pioneered individual tutoring of young children as the most effective way of promoting concentration and systematic learning. The method involves each child spending 20 minutes each day withdrawn from the group, in close one-to-one interaction with the teacher.

This approach has the advantage of taking as a starting point the child's own interests and development in a way which a prescribed structured programme cannot; at the same time because of the one to one teaching situation, the teacher is able to follow-up questions in order to probe the child, help him formulate the solution to a problem, in a way which would not be possible in the normal group of children all seeking attention simultaneously.

The West Riding team recognized the artificiality of introducing a programme as a 'package deal' or a 'shot-in-the-arm'. They were reluctant even to adopt one approach to the education of pre-school children; the keynote of their work was its diversity. They argue (Smith, 1975) that taking one approach fails to recognize the multitude of other experiences which may affect the child's assimilation of the content of the particular programme. For this reason, the individual work was conceived of as but one level in the design of the pre-school experience. A second level was that of group work, more akin to the normal nursery programme, except that it was felt necessary to ensure that the child could use the materials provided in the individual sessions to practice the skills learned and generalize them to new situations. This contrasts with the introduction of PLDK, where there was a clear dichotomy between Peabody time and the rest of the day.

As well as affording opportunities to reinforce the skills learned in the individual sessions, the group situation was considered to develop other skills in its own right. In particular it provided the basis for imaginative games involving the use of language in role playing. In this respect the team were influenced by the work of Sara Smilansky in Israel (Smilansky, 1968).

Finally the West Riding team took account in their planning of the wider context of the child's experiences, the relation of nursery experiences to life at home. This approach reveals the perspective of the programme which seeks to complement rather than compensate for the home. Consequently the team decided that a half-day programme of concentrated educational experiences would be of more advantage to the children than a full day programme. They were also concerned not to suggest that the nursery was taking over the role of parents as educators, and endeavoured at all times to involve the parents in the work of the nursery groups. More of this will be described in a subsequent chapter (VI).

In essence, then, the difference between this programme and the PLDK was that it aimed to complement rather than compensate for children's home experiences by providing diverse types of activity within an integrated nursery day (or more correctly half-day), rather than 20 minutes of structured programme tagged onto an otherwise informal programme of free-play. This model offers more possibilities for future development. In the long term the nurseries involved in the NFER and EPA projects have not continued to use the PLDK in its entirety; at most the nurseries have drawn on the materials and used them with small groups, but integrated within the nursery day.

(ii) *'Dr. Wotever' — (Liverpool EPA)*

'Dr. Wotever' was one part of a series of curriculum development projects carried out by the Liverpool team for all stages of education and described in Midwinter (1972). They all arose out of the concept of 'community education', with an emphasis on making the school curriculum relevant to the child's out-of-school experiences.

Specifically, 'Dr. Wotever' developed out of dissatisfaction with the American idiom of the Peabody Kit, and a suspicion that the style of presentation of activities was likely to alienate many children as much as did the traditional primary school programme to which the project team paid most of their attention.

The importance of the 'Dr. Wotever' programme lies more in the rationale and purpose than in the product of the development work. The Liverpool team were working mostly within playgroups, many set up as a result of their efforts, and they wanted to provide a programme which might encourage playgroup staffs to follow a more systematic procedure to foster language development which made fullest use of the opportunities provided by the locality. The Kit was based on a core vocabulary of 360 words which national norms and local testing suggested should be familiar to playgroup children. A further 360 words were also selected which were to be introduced to the children. Twenty-four stories were then written using the vocabulary and successively introducing items from the 'new' vocabulary list. Like the PLDK, the Kit used a puppet presenter, Dr. Wotever and centred on a local block of flats, their inhabitants and caretaker, and told of the experiences of two small boys. Midwinter (1972) reports the Kit as being received enthusiastically by the playgroups involved.

(iii) *Intensification of good nursery practice (Deptford EPA)*

Of all the projects discussed here, the Deptford EPA team were most critically aware of the conflict between the methods of the PLDK and the recognized 'good practices' of nursery education. Indeed the team report that the nursery class teachers with whom they were working did not wish to take part in the national experiment (Barnes, 1975, p. 71).

For this reason, the emphasis of the team's work was on co-operating with teachers to develop methods by which language could be fostered within the context of their normal nursery practices, described in further detail in (Barnes, 1975, part 4).

(iv) *A general pre-school programme (Dundee EPA).*

The Dundee team faced similar problems to the Deptford team.

They found themselves unable to participate in the national evaluation of PLDK because of nursery teachers' reluctance to permit introduction of a structured Kit into the nursery. As a result the team developed and evaluated their own British programme in collaboration with a working party of local teachers. The programme was designed to ensure systematic use of play activities to promote children's learning, and adopted a thematic approach. Each week a new overall theme was introduced to the children to be illustrated and developed in a daily 'playsem' (a play-seminar of about eight children). In their report the research team described the programme as not differing greatly from normal nursery activities, the only difference being a slight increase in the amount of 'direction' given to children, although as far as possible the direction operated through the organization of the activities and situation. The emphasis was still on the child learning through his own efforts:

> 'Instead of creating a situation in which one of many discoveries is "possible" for a child — a whole series of linked situations is created in which a particular discovery becomes highly "probable".'
> (Morrison, Watt and Lee, 1974, p. 33)

The programme was intended to allow the teacher a great deal of flexibility in her use of the themes and their presentation to the children. Over 50 themes were developed through more than 200 playsems covering the following general concepts: Number, Size, Quantity, Equivalence, Shape, Space Position and Body Image.

Nevertheless, the research team recognized the inherent danger of a flexible and informal approach which makes it difficult for teachers to monitor the programme and the children's progress. Similar problems were experienced by the research teams evaluating other non-directive programmes. In all cases the problem has been resolved, at least in part, by devising a simple checklist, completed by the teachers, which provided a profile of the range of concepts to be developed by the programme.

III. Programmes of cognitive development

The main emphasis of British compensatory work has been on language. This reflects its undoubted importance for the child's school success but also resulted from the interest in language development amongst social scientists. Aspects of child language were one of the major pre-occupations of psychologists, sociologists and educationists during the 1960s. This research has provided a wealth of data from which hypotheses could be derived about the origins of educational failure and the type of programme appropriate to improving language skills. Nevertheless other aspects of cognitive functioning have not been totally neglected, and programmes have been developed and evaluated to improve perceptual and conceptual abilities.

(i) *The Perceptual Programme (NFER)*

The NFER perceptual programme was introduced to complement the Peabody Kit (Woodhead, 1976, Chap. 4). The intention was to encourage general perceptual and motor skills, but especially those which might contribute to a child's later success in learning to read. All the children who experienced the PLDK also took part in activities designed to develop perceptual skills. The decision to use the PLDK had determined the style of presentation of the language programme, namely small specially withdrawn groups. No such constraints operated for the perceptual programme, which the NFER team adapted to the methods already existing in the nursery schools. The perceptual programme took advantage of various situations to introduce materials and activities.

There has always been a tradition of perceptual training in the nursery and many of the materials to be found in the well-equipped nursery schools have their origins in the pioneering work by Maria Montessori. The NFER team took advantage of these resources. Consequently a major component of the programme consisted of classroom activities.

Design of the classroom activities was guided by a classification into six general areas: use of crayons and drawing; co-ordination activities; use of constructional toys; use of jigsaws, matching and sorting activities; cutting out and pasting; and painting through various media. This classification was drawn up as a result of discussions with nursery staff and it was of considerable importance in guiding the day to day administration of the programme in the informal atmosphere of the nursery day. Subsequently, a simple checklist was derived from the classification and used by staff to monitor children's progress. The classroom activities relied heavily on already existing nursery equipment. Some additional published games and activities were also included where these were designed to achieve specific objectives (e.g. matching and sorting games).

Although the Peabody Kit is called a 'language' programme many of the activities train much more general abilities, especially where language serves to mediate perceptual activities (e.g. relational concepts and discrimination ability). Recognizing the potential value of presenting these tasks in a more structured situation than the normal classroom, the NFER team supplemented these by extra activities especially designed by the project with materials illustrated by an artist.

(ii) *The Concept Development Programme (Birmingham EPA)*

The Birmingham team were responsible for introducing a programme to develop numerical concepts (Halsey, 1972). The theoretical background for this concept-development programme was provided by Piaget's account of the processes underlying numerical ability. The specific focus of the programme was on the conservation of number. Although Piaget's work has had a considerable impact on research in development psychology and the content of training courses for teachers, relatively less interest has been shown by those interested in disadvantage and compensatory education. This stems largely from Piaget's own reluctance to discuss the origins of differences between children. The main emphasis of his work has been to describe what he believes to be the invariant sequence of stages through which every child passes, although some a little later than others. Additionally his theoretical framework argues that the origins of development lie in the child's interaction with the physical environment. Little emphasis is placed on the role of teaching, and the development of language is not seen as intimately related to, or as a determinant of, conceptual growth. Piaget's colleague, Sinclair-de-Zwart, has been particularly responsible for developing this argument and substantiating it with research results (Sinclair-de-Zwart, 1969).

Although the Piagetian tradition would not predict that training would have any significance for the improvement in performance of disadvantaged children, these arguments have not passed unchallenged. In particular Bruner, Olver and Greenfield (1966) have been responsible for comparing the development of the concept of conservation in Western children with that of the Kpelle of Liberia in West Africa and arguing that observed variations reflect differences in the children's experience of using language as an instructional tool; the children who have received Western-style education appear to develop the concept at roughly the same time as English children.

The particular research which influenced the development of the Birmingham EPA's programme was conducted by J.G. Wallace and J. Mason and the programme prepared by J. Mason and W.D. Clarke. This research had suggested that conceptual development could be accelerated, especially when the programme included non-verbal methods.

The programme relied largely on making use of materials already available in the nurseries. A manual was prepared which specified the content of a large number of units designed to teach numerical concepts. The manual was used flexibly by the teachers to fit in with the activities of the normal nursery day.

Conclusions

These then are the seven approaches to pre-school intervention which were tried out by the EPA and NFER research teams. They differ both in focus and style. Most energy has been invested on strategies to improve children's verbal skills, with rather less emphasis on perceptual or conceptual development. Variations in style have depended on the extent to which programmes have departed from traditional informal methods in favour of more formal structured teaching strategies. However, leaving aside these superficial differences the programmes were all united by two common general features.

In all cases promoting aspects of cognitive learning has been emphasized more than any other aspects of development. The other aspects have been neglected not because they were considered unimportant but because the research teams believed that the nursery was already catering adequately for physical, social and emotional development. The emphasis on cognitive programmes was justified also on the grounds that this is the crucial factor determining whether children are adequately prepared for the demands of later schooling.

The other common feature is related. For effective learning to take place the organization of the nursery programme must be systematic. Underlying all these programmes was the desire to enhance the learning environment of the nursery either by a formal systematic method or by sensitizing teachers to the importance of planning for an informal nursery programme and making educationally-purposeful interventions in children's activities.

None of these could be described as 'model programmes'. They were a mixture of language kits taken "off the shelf" and tentative innovations made in the classroom. Undoubtedly, in Britain today there will be examples of nursery practices which are better planned, more systematic, adapted more appropriately to the characteristics of the children, and in every other way vastly superior to the programmes described here. The only reason for dwelling at such length on these particular programmes is because they are not just examples of different approaches to intervention through the nursery. They also have the virtue of having been submitted to systematic evaluation; 'action' was complemented by 'research'.

The value of this type of action-research is not that specific intervention programmes are likely to have any lasting merit. These projects were designed as experiments, to discover what is the potential of various strategies for improving the subsequent attainments of children. The evaluation of these programmes is prefaced by the question: 'What *can* be achieved through intervention in the nursery?'.

Chapter IV

What can be achieved through intervention in the nursery?

The purpose of evaluation studies

So far we have described the circumstances in which special nursery programmes have been developed and introduced. By contrast, the main emphasis of this section will be on the research evidence for their success, and the implications which the projects may have for future developments. Inevitably this will require entering into the world of research techniques and terms, a world which is not noted for being self-explanatory or jargon-free. As far as possible the rationale for the design of the evaluations will be explained as the discussion proceeds.

The research results provide evidence bearing on three principal issues:

(1) What is the effectiveness of a special nursery programme in improving children's abilities?

(2) Which type of nursery programme is most effective in improving children's abilities?

(3) What are the long-term effects of a special programme on children's later attainment and adjustment in the infant school?

It will be as well to make clear at the outset that the results we shall report offer few clear-cut answers to these questions. If taken at face-value they may seem to offer solutions, but there are plenty of good reasons for exercising caution before jumping to the apparently 'obvious' conclusions. In common with all research, the results obtained are not a direct reflection of the nature of the phenomena we are studying. They depend very considerably on the way the research questions were posed and the methods that were adopted to study them.

This is particularly true of this type of research which has direct educational, social and political implications. The research questions did not arise solely out of academic interests and were not amenable to the type of controlled experimentation and refined measurement procedures which are possible in the research scientist's laboratory. Inevitably then, the results cannot be interpreted as 'cut-and-dried' solutions to educational issues. To do so might make the text more readable and decision-making simpler, but it would also be a mis-representation of what the studies really tell us. Accordingly, in the account which follows simple interpretations of the results have been sacrificed in favour of a more complex account which also recognizes shortcomings in the research methodology, and throws doubt on the usefulness of some of the research questions which were posed.

The account is divided into three sections corresponding to the main types of question outlined above. The main sources for the review are the five volumes of *Educational Priority* and the report of the 'Pre-School Project'.

(1) The main effects of a special programme

There are numerous questions subsumed under this general heading which have been investigated by research methods:

> What is the effect on children's abilities of experiencing a special programme to supplement normal nursery activities? Does the programme affect any other aspects of children's functioning, notably social development and emotional adjustment? Does the age at which a child begins the programme and the number of terms he experiences it affect the benefits he may derive? Do some children benefit more than others from the special programme; does the programme serve to close the 'ability-gap' between advantaged and disadvantaged groups?

Of all the programmes described in the previous chapter, the Peabody Language Development Kit has been most extensively intro-duced and rigourously evaluated. Consequently this first set of questions will be discussed by reference almost exclusively to this kit. Although the programmes used by the EPA and NFER teams differed slightly, NFER having adapted the Peabody Kit, the design of the evaluations was sufficiently similar to justify treatment together. This is summarized in Table I.

Design of the evaluation studies

The research design was a product of compromise between the ideal requirements of research and the practical realities of the nursery

Table 1: Design of the main evaluation studies

Context	Groups	Numbers	Pre-Test	Intevention	Post-Test
EPA Project: Nursery Classes Playgroups	Control	128	EPVT RDLS	Normal nursery programme (3 Terms)	EPVT RDLS
	Experimental	128	EPVT RDLS	Normal nursery programme plus Peabody Kit (3 Terms)	EPVT RDLS
NFER Project:	Control	117	EPVT ITPA (5 sub-tests) Eisenberg (2 Scales)	Normal nursery programme (1–6 terms)	EPVT ITPA (5 sub-tests) Eisenberg (2 scales) Effectiveness— Motivation Scale
Nursery Schools	Experimental	155	EPVT ITPA (5 sub-tests) Eisenberg (2 Scales)	Normal nursery programme plus Peabody Kit (1–6 Terms)	EPVT ITPA (5 sub-tests) Eisenberg (2 scales) Effectiveness— Motivation Scale

setting. In most cases, it was not possible to assign children from the same population randomly to a control group (who experienced 'normal' nursery activities only) and an experimental group (who additionally experienced the Peabody programme). The best that was achieved was to endeavour to match groups according to social background and nursery experience. The circumstances of individual nurseries determined the details of the design.

The NFER evaluation was conducted with three- and four-year-old children in four nursery schools in Slough. Two of the schools provided children for the programme group only; one provided control children only; and the fourth provided children for both groups. Two hundred and seventy-two children were involved in the evaluation; approximately half of these experienced the programme for between one and five or six terms. It was considered important that the children who would be most likely to benefit should experience the programme; consequently nearly half of the experimental children were selected from those who had been admitted to the nursery full-time on grounds of social need. Although this was not reflected in differences in initial scores on the criterion measures (of verbal ability etc.), it was to affect the interpretation of results throughout the study.

The EPA teams experienced considerable problems in designing a controlled evaluation within the context of three different areas (Birmingham, Liverpool and West Riding) and two types of nursery. The programme was introduced in two nursery classes admitting children full-time, two nursery classes admitting children part-time and three playgroups. Control groups were selected from other similar nurseries, as far as possible in the same area, with the exception of one part-time nursery class in the West Riding (experimental) which was matched with a similar unit in Liverpool (control). This immediately raised a problem of ensuring that the normal nursery experience of experimental and control groups was comparable. This was not so serious for the NFER project since all the children were selected from schools from the same area administered by the same LEA. As a precaution the EPA teams asked an HMI to visit all the nurseries and, with the help of LEA advisers, make assessments of aspects of the nursery which would influence the quality of educational experiences being offered to the children (e.g. premises, equipment, staff qualifications etc.). Overall, no major discrepancies were found between experimental and control nurseries.

In all, 128 experimental and 128 control children were selected for the main EPA evaluation. Both groups of children came from similar home backgrounds and were considered likely to benefit from a special programme. Consequently there was no problem of unmatched groups. The EPA programme was evaluated over a one year period.

In both the NFER and EPA projects the children were allowed to settle into the normal nursery before being introduced to the special programme. The programme was administered to small groups of children for approximately 20 minutes each day, in the case of the EPA groups by a member of the nursery staff. The NFER programme was taught by the headmistress of one of the schools, by a member of the research team and by a teacher specially seconded by the LEA.

Both projects relied for their evaluation on the comparison of experimental and control groups in terms of the amount of improvement in verbal ability during the course of their nursery experience. However the instruments used as criteria of improvement differed slightly.

Both project teams chose a simply administered measure of vocabulary, the English Picture Vocabulary Test (EPVT), Pre-School and Level I (Brimer and Dunn, 1962). This is an English version of an American test, the Peabody Picture Vocabulary Test, which measures receptive vocabulary (i.e. the ability to select from a choice of four pictures the one which most closely represents a word spoken by the tester).

The projects differed in their choice of a principal language measure. NFER chose five sub-tests of an American instrument, the Illinois Test of Psycholinguistic Abilities (ITPA), developed by Kirk, McCarthy and Kirk (1968). The instrument seemed most appropriate to the evaluation of the kit; it had been developed from the same model of psycholinguistic processes (namely that developed by Osgood, 1957) and covered more than specific language skills to include general verbal abilities. The ITPA sub-tests chosen were designed to assess children's knowledge of grammatical structure, their ability to describe simple objects, make meaningful associations within groups of words and pictures, and their auditory memory. The disadvantage of the test was that only American 'norms' were available. The EPA teams selected the Reynell Developmental Language Scales (RDLS, Reynell, 1969) 'as the only purely language tests for pre-school children for which English norms had been established' (Halsey, 1972, page 91). The test produced two scores, of verbal comprehension and of expressive language. These tests were administered to children individually by an experienced tester.

Effects of the programme on children's verbal performance

The NFER results on the EPVT and ITPA demonstrate the considerable advances children had made following experience of the special programme. Figure 1 illustrates the finding that although both groups had improved their scores after nursery experience, the gain made by the special programme group was significantly greater than

Figure 1: Peabody Language Development Kit — the NFER Results

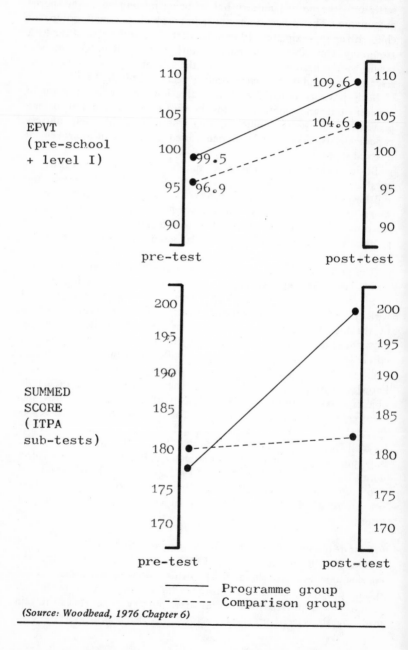

EPVT
(pre-school
+ level I)

SUMMED
SCORE
(ITPA
sub-tests)

—————— Programme group
- - - - - - Comparison group

(Source: Woodhead, 1976 Chapter 6)

**Figure 2: Peabody Language Development Kit — the EPA results
(An illustration for three nursery groups in Birmingham)**

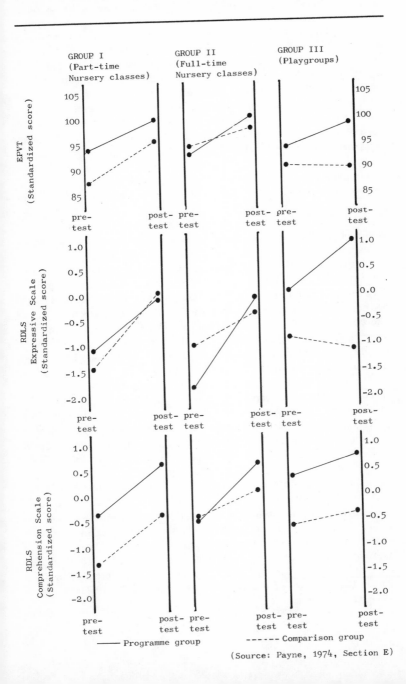

(Source: Payne, 1974, Section E)

that by the control group. This was also the pattern for each of the ITPA sub-tests treated separately, which is indicative that the beneficial effects of the special programme have been general across a wide range of aspects of verbal performance.

The results of the EPA evaluation are less striking and appear to vary between nurseries. Very few of the differences between experimental and control groups were statistically significant, which has been interpreted as due to the small numbers in each sub-group (Halsey, 1972, p.94). But the pattern of results is quite revealing and suggests some of the limitations of this type of intervention and evaluation. For simplicity, the results are illustrated (Figure 2) for three pairs of nursery groups in one area only (Birmingham). The results for the other areas were quite similar (Halsey, 1972, pp.92—3; Payne, 1974, section E).

Looking first at differences between experimental and control groups, the results suggest that the Peabody Kit has been effective in some types of nursery (i.e. Group III), but not in others (i.e. Group I). To fully understand the reasons for this apparent differential effectiveness of the programme we need to look separately at the pattern of changes in score of the experimental groups and the control groups.

The trend for the experimental groups is consistent. Although the magnitude of gain differs, in all cases average scores have improved between pre- and post-testing. The trend for the control groups is much less consistent. In Group I no difference was found between programme and control groups; both had shown considerable and parallel improvement since pre-testing. Control Group II also improved, although not as much as the programme group. By contrast, Control Group III actually deteriorated on two out of the three measures.

The explanation for the apparent differential effectiveness of the special programme appears to lie in two factors: differences in the level of commitment of the staff to the aims and methods of the programme as well as their skill in administering it; and differences in the quality of the 'normal' nursery environment experienced by the control groups.

Not all of the staff in the experimental nurseries adopted the Peabody Kit with wholehearted enthusiasm. The reservations expressed by some of them have been described in Chapter III. Interpreting the EPA results, Halsey notes that the teacher who was least enthusiastic about the Kit seemed to have transmitted her lack of enthusiasm to the children; the children she taught made almost the smallest improvements of any group (Halsey, 1972, p. 96). The discovery that the attitudes of a teacher to an educational method are crucial to its success is a familiar one to researchers (for example, notably illustrated by Joan Barker-Lunn's study of streaming in the primary school (Barker-Lunn, 1970)).

The differential commitment and skill of staff may very well explain the differences in amount of gain by the children who experienced the special programme. As further support it may be recalled that the commitment of the teachers of the NFER programme was considerable; one had been seconded specially for the job, the two others had been responsible for the English revision of the manual. A related possibility is that the greater gains by children in the NFER evaluation are not due to the programme at all but to the increased staff-child ratios which resulted from the presence of the special teacher and the member of the research team who administered the programme. It is not possible to test this, except to note that the improvements were just as great in the one nursery where the PLDK was taught for the most part by a member of the staff, the headmistress.

The other influence on the effectiveness of the PLDK seems to be the quality of the nursery in which it is introduced and with which it is compared. The rationale for making a comparison between the programme and normal nursery experience, assumes that there is some norm of nursery practices on which the special programme can build and with which it can be compared. The EPA results throw doubt on the validity of this assumption. The divergent trends for the three control groups illustrated are clear evidence that the normal nursery programme experienced by these children are of a very different quality: Groups I, and to a lesser extent II, provide a programme which promotes language development; Group III does not.

It must not be assumed that the programme in Groups II and III is of an inferior quality in all respects; the work of the staff may be directed towards attaining other than .language objectives for the children. It must also be emphasized that this comparison does not permit conclusions to be drawn about the relative merits of 'normal' programmes provided by different types of establishment. When all the EPA groups are considered together, there is no consistent trend for the normal programme of one type of establishment to produce greater gains in attainment than other establishments.

Much more important than the type of establishment is likely to be the effort made by staff to improve children's language abilities. In cases like Group I where the staff are already sensitive to the importance of encouraging language skills the control group have gained as much as the experimental group. This conclusion was supported by the ratings of the HMI. Both the nurseries in Group I were rated very highly.

The greatest merit of a special programme like PLDK appears to be its ability to produce consistent improvements in language ability in all nurseries, whether or not the facilities are good and the staff are highly qualified. This was true for all seven of the EPA nurseries which used the programme.

In short, these results suggest that a special programme can have a consistently beneficial effect in improving the language performance of children in various types of nursery. However whether this effect is greater than that achieved by the normal nursery programme will depend very considerably on the quality of the educational environment already being provided, and on the level of commitment and skill of the staff who use the special programme.

Effects of a special programme on children's behaviour and adjustment

In addition to the measures of language ability, NFER also included in the pre-test/post-test battery, assessments of children's classroom behaviour, social development and emotional adjustment. The rationale for including these instruments was the fears which had been expressed that however beneficial the PLDK might be for children's language attainment, experience of a structured programme of this kind would be detrimental to the normal progress of other aspects of their development. The classroom behaviour measures were all in the form of rating scales to be completed by the teachers. They consisted of a series of descriptions of child behaviour to be rated for their appropriateness to the individual child. Two measures were administered before and after children had experienced the programme. Both were developed in the USA by Eisenberg (1962); the 'Symptom Checklist' describes symptoms of disturbed behaviour and the 'Health Inventory' positive traits exhibited in the child's behaviour as an individual, in the group and in relation to the nursery staff. One further instrument was administered on post-test only, the 'Effectiveness Motivation Scale' developed by Stott and Sharp (Stott, Williams and Sharp, 1976), which described the child's behaviour in 11 familiar nursery settings.

Interpretation of the results on these scales is complicated by incomplete data and differences in style of rating between teachers. But generally the results did not suggest the special programme had any different effect on the children than normal nursery experience (Woodhead, 1976, Chapter 6).

Can intervention programmes reduce inequalities in attainment?

In the discussions which form the background to these projects, one of the key themes was the possibility of using early education to reduce educational, and ultimately social, inequalities. The special nursery programmes which were subsequently introduced had been designed as particularly suitable for children from disadvantaged homes who might suffer retarded language development (Dunn *et al.*, 1968).

The NFER evaluation of the Peabody Kit took account of this special purpose for the programme. In addition to making an assessment of the main effects of the programme for all children, taking average scores for the complete group, the effects were also analysed after the groups had been subdivided according to characteristics of their home environment. The most important subdivision was by social class (based on parental occupation). Social class is both predictive of differences in children's abilities and school attainment, and is also the principal concept used in most sociological theory of social structure and organization. If special programmes in the nursery could be shown to reduce social class differences this would have major repercussions not only for educational theory and practice but also for social policy.

In practice the findings of the research do not point to the special programmes having potential as a miraculous panacea for social or educational inequalities. The NFER project found that the social class differences in verbal ability which were apparent before the programme was introduced persisted until children were re-tested when they left the nursery (Fig. 3).

This result has been repeated in other American evaluations (reviewed by Bronfenbrenner, 1973). Indeed a number of the evaluators (e.g. Herzog *et al.*, 1972) have reported that, if anything, it is the more advantaged children who gain most from a special programme.

Not surprisingly perhaps, exposure to a special programme appears to benefit all children, but especially those who are more able and receptive from the start. On this basis, the provision of nursery education for all children would not be a road to equality of attainment. There is, however, one condition under which special programmes might be used to this end, which would require selecting only the disadvantaged groups to receive the special treatment. The NFER evaluation provides some evidence to support this conclusion. If children from lower social class who experienced the special programme are compared with children from higher social class who experienced normal nursery education only, initial differences in test scores are markedly reduced although they still remain significantly different.

To put the implication of this result into practical effect would require exercising positive discrimination in favour of children from low social class or with low ability. This could be achieved in a number of ways. At the simplest level, if nursery education were only made available to these groups, then some measure of equality of attainment might in principle be achieved by the time all children entered compulsory education. This philosophy of positive discrimination provides part of the rationale for concentrating resources in the underprivileged areas, particularly in our largest cities, a policy advocated by Plowden, and put into practice under the Urban Aid Scheme. However, recent policy statements (notably the 1972 White Paper) have recommended making nursery provision much more

Figure 3: Social class and programme effects (NFER project)

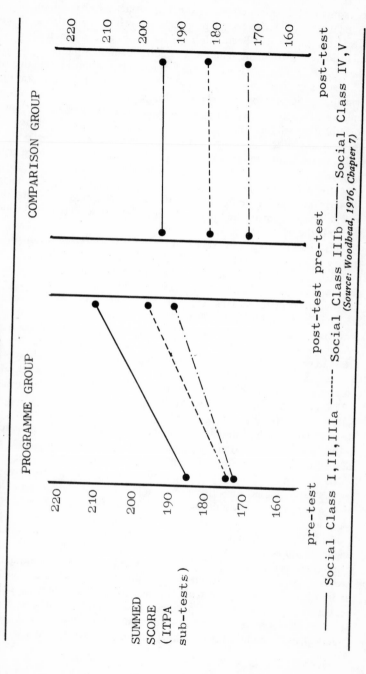

SUMMED
SCORE
(ITPA
sub-tests)

(Source: Woodhead, 1976, Chapter 7)

——— Social Class I, II, IIIa ------- Social Class IIIb —·—·— Social Class IV, V

generally available. In this eventuality, a policy of positive discrimination could only operate within the framework of a nursery programme provided for all children. Withdrawal of the most needy children to engage in a special programme of language training might prove an effective method of ensuring that all children went on to primary education already in command of the basic verbal and cognitive skills.

It must be emphasized that the findings which have been described are specific to the circumstances surrounding individual research projects. The evaluations have not shown especially beneficial effects of a special programme to disadvantaged children, but this may be a result of the limitations of the programme or the way it was introduced. It was not the programme alone which was being evaluated by these projects, but the skill of the teacher in using it, adapting it to individual children, and making sure that each child was progressing without neglecting one for another. The conclusion should not be that the special programme has failed to serve the children for whom it was intended. Rather, we need to examine much more closely alternative strategies which might produce even greater improvements in performance, and discover optimal circumstances in which they might be introduced.

Does longer programme-experience produce bigger gains in test score?

The main evaluation established that a special programme can produce improvements in test score which are significantly greater than those resulting from normal nursery experience. Many of the subsidiary analyses which have been conducted were designed to explore in more detail the precise pattern of effects in relation to a number of other factors.

One of the more important questions which was tackled by the NFER team and the Dundee EPA team, concerns the relationship between the number of terms children experienced the programme and the magnitude of its effects. Both teams came to the conclusion that the relationship is not linear. Some of the results of the NFER analysis are presented as Figure 4. Within the programme group, children did not improve significantly more after four or more terms' experience than after only one term's experience.

The Dundee team interpret the result as pointing to the inadequacy of the programme, which they argue reflects our own lack of understanding of the most appropriate points in a child's development for introducing particular educational stimuli (Morrison, Watt and Lee, 1974, p.158). Certainly, the results which have been obtained are specific to this particular programme introduced in these particular

Figure 4: Length of experience and programme effectiveness (NFER project)

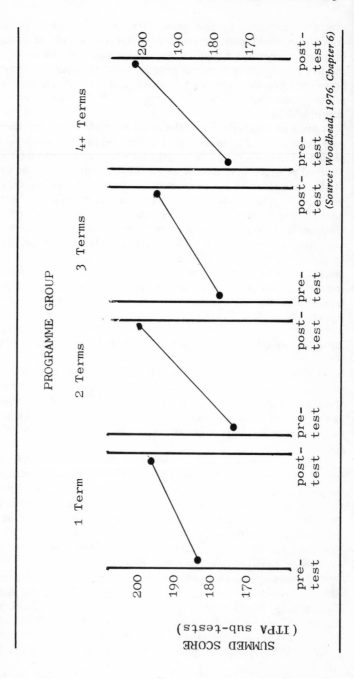

(Source: Woodhead, 1976, Chapter 6)

circumstances.

Injection of the intensive educational experiences appears to have an immediate boosting effect. The failure to show subsequent improvements may imply either that the programme used lacked sufficient development to 'stretch' the children, or rapidly became too advanced for them. Either way there can be no final conclusion on the issue. It will depend entirely on such factors as the content of the particular programme, how it is taught, to whom it is taught, and how its effectiveness is evaluated. It may well be possible to design a programme which could produce the cumulative effects which everyone would like to see.

One problem with this evaluation is that it does not disentangle the influence of two important factors. In the NFER analysis, age of starting and length of experience of the programme were confounded; the children who experienced the programme for the longest duration also began it at the youngest age. The result might merely reflect the inappropriateness of the programme to the youngest groups of children rather than the failure of the programme to show cumulative benefits. On the other hand, it has been argued that what matters for the success of an intervention is the age at which it commences — the earlier the better (Bronfenbrenner, 1973).

The influence of these two variables has not been adequately separated in any British study. Such studies have, however, been conducted by Karnes (1973) as part of the programme of the University of Illinois Institute for Research on Exceptional Children. In one study children were introduced to a programme at four-years-old and their progress monitored through subsequent years of programme experience. Periodic measures on the Stanford-Binet intelligence scale showed that initial gains after the equivalent of two to three terms were of much greater magnitude than subsequent gains after the equivalent of six or more terms. In another study one group of three-year-olds and one group of four-year-olds were administered the same programme (adapted to the developmental level of the two groups). When re-tested after one year, the groups were found to have made comparable gains in score.

It seems that we cannot avoid the inescapable conclusion that despite being designed as a carefully sequenced programme of language training, the Peabody Kit has only succeeded in producing an initial boost in scores. The most probable interpretation is that the effectiveness of the programme is not due to its specific content, but some more general effect of increasing children's familiarity with verbal tasks, and providing them with experience of working in a close instructional relationship with an adult. This need not necessarily be considered as evidence that the programme has failed. A more useful interpretation of the results might be that nursery children currently lack experience of instructional situations which, if provided, could quite quickly boost their performance in verbal tasks.

In fact there is evidence that the effectiveness of a programme like Peabody is a product both of its specific content and also its general character. This conclusion can be drawn from comparisons which have been made of the effectiveness of programmes with different teaching content and different teaching method. This is one of the subjects of the next section.

(2) Comparisons of the effectiveness of special programmes

So far the discussion has been restricted to evaluations of the Peabody Kit. Although it has been most extensively evaluated, this is not the only special programme for which research data are available. It is now appropriate to make a comparison between these results and those obtained for the other programmes which were described in the previous chapter.

Each of these programmes was evaluated in its own right. But the emphasis here will be on what light these evaluations throw on the reasons for the success of a special programme. The following detailed questions are pertinent:

Are other aspects of children's development besides language amenable to the same type of rapid improvement as a result of a special programme?

Is the success of the special programme due to its specific language content, or the more general benefits of following a structured method in the nursery?

Would alternative methods be as successful in promoting language development?

The effects of a language versus a perceptual programme

The evaluation of the NFER's perceptual programme (described on page 36 provides some evidence on the first question. The design of the evaluation was the same as for Peabody. The perceptual programme was administered concurrently with the Peabody Kit to the same group of children. In addition to the language measures children were pre-and post-tested on a battery of five perceptual instruments. This design enabled the team to establish whether children would benefit from perceptual as well as language training (Woodhead, 1976, chap 6).

Generally speaking the results did not show improvements on the perceptual measures comparable with those on the language measures, a finding which can be interpreted in a number of ways. It may mean that perceptual abilities are not so easily modified as verbal skills, or alternatively that the instruments used to evaluate the programme were inappropriate and did not reflect the content of the training. But perhaps the most plausible hypothesis is that traditional nursery practices, which have always included activities with a major perceptual component, already provide sufficient experiences relevant to these skills and do not need to be supplemented by a special programme. Unfortunately, in the absence of norms for most of the measures it is not possible to test this hypothesis fully. But certainly in the case of the ITPA sub-test for which norms are available, both groups seem to have improved as a result of their nursery experience. In conclusion, the importance of perceptual abilities for later school success is not doubted, but there does not seem to be the need to introduce a special programme; the normal nursery is already providing a considerable number of activities to promote perceptual development.

Are programme effects due to specific content or general method?

Data collected in the evaluation of Birmingham EPA's Concept Development Programme (page 37) provides an explanation for the 'booster' effect described in the last section (page 53). Although the objectives were different the teaching methods adopted in this programme were quite similar to those used in the Peabody programme, requiring intensive small group instruction. By examining the improvements in language development made by children after experiencing the concept programme the team hoped to establish whether the effects of Peabody were due to the intensive method or the specific 'language' content.

Accordingly, the children who experienced the concept programme were a different group from those who experienced the language programme. Nevertheless, both groups, as well as children who only experienced the normal nursery programme were assessed on the language measures as well as a measure of concept development. This measure of concept development used the procedure developed by Piaget to assess conservation of number, namely comparing rows of items spaced out or close together with the questions 'Which has more?', 'Which has the most?' and 'Why?'.

Comparing the three groups on this conceptual measure showed a clear effect of the programme on children's development. On commencement of the programme children showed poor conservation of number, and little change was observed by the end of the programme for the PLDK and normal nursery group. By contrast, Halsey (1972) reports that the number group showed great improvement in all but one playgroup, where the staff had found it difficult to arrange regular administration of the programme.

When the crucial comparison was made between the groups on the measures of language development the results suggested that the increased staff attention entailed by the concept programme did indeed have beneficial effects for the children's language development. The improvements of children who had experienced the concept-development programme were greater than the normal nursery group although not as great as the Peabody group. Halsey (1972, p. 98) interprets this result as indicative that there are two components to the benefits children were found to derive from the Peabody Kit: a general programme effect, and one specific to the content of the programme.

This finding of the Birmingham EPA team suggests that we cannot expect to find some miraculous formula for a language development programme. Any intensive programme, which entails a high level of verbal interaction between adults and children is likely to have the effect of improving the children's language, even if it was not designed for that particular purpose.

Which type of programme is most effective?

Leaving aside these incidental benefits of a nursery programme, we must now consider research evidence for the relative merits of various programmes which have been designed with language development as their principal objective. The purpose of the exercise is to discover which is the most effective *method* of improving pre-school children's verbal abilities: is intensive small group formal instruction more effective than individual tutoring or a thematic method integrated in the normal programme?

It will be recalled from the previous chapter that there were four 'alternative language programmes': 'The Individual Language Programme' (West Riding EPA), 'Dr. Wotever' (Liverpool EPA), 'Intensification of Good Nursery Practice' (Deptford EPA), and 'A General Pre-School Programme' (Dundee EPA). Of these, we can eliminate 'Dr. Wotever' which was not systematically evaluated.

The West Riding team designed an evaluation to compare the effectiveness of two programmes involving quite closely structured intensive language teaching: one was the group teaching method of the Peabody Language Development Kit, the other the tutoring method of the Individual Language Programme (page 32). Generally speaking, both special groups made greater improvements between pre-and post-testing than a 'normal' nursery group. But the results did not point to one programme as being more effective than another; instead a pattern of differential effects on children's abilities was observed. There were certain aspects of verbal ability on which each special programme group showed much greater improvement than either the other special or the normal nursery group. In particular the Peabody Kit produced high scores on the assessments of vocabulary, and the Individual programme appeared best suited to developing children's knowledge of complex grammatical structure. This pattern of differential effects is discussed in greater detail by Smith (1975, p. 110).

The Dundee and Deptford teams did not participate in the main EPA evaluation of the Peabody Language Development Kit. Their research was designed to assess the effect on children's abilities of a language programme based on and integrated within a normal nursery programme (pp. 34—5). Both teams found that children who experienced this programme made gains in verbal ability (which were very substantial in the case of the Dundee project). However, in both cases, these gains were very closely paralleled by gains observed for the control (normal nursery) group. For a complete account of these evaluations the reader is referred to Morrison, 1974, Chap. 10; and Barnes, 1975, Chap. 5. The results point to the failure of the teaching methods incorporated in these special programmes to make any impact on children's abilities over and above the effects of the normal nursery programme.

However, interpretation of the implications of these results is fraught with problems similar to those described in the first section of this chapter (p. 47). The basic flaw in the research design of these projects is the failure to control adequately the nursery experience of the group with whom the special programme was being compared. Of course this was essentially a practical problem; control of the 'normal' nursery programme would not have been feasible. Nevertheless, the failure to do so has had major repercussions. It is extremely difficult to interpret whether differences in the amount of improvement shown by experimental and control groups reflect the 'excellence' of the special programme or the 'mediocrity' of the normal nursery programme. We may suspect that the lack of difference for the Dundee programme was due to the high quality of the already existing programme; the size of the gains made are evidence of this. Compared with a different 'control' group, this programme might have been shown to be highly effective. In the absence of an adequate characterization of the 'normal' nursery programme, the British results do not permit us to make a firm judgement on this issue. However, the fact that it is only on the two more structured intensive language programmes that significant differences were found in the improvements made by the two groups does suggest some feature common to both programmes as having the greatest potential. Such a conclusion is supported by the more comprehensive and controlled evaluations which have been conducted in the USA.

A project directed by Karnes (1973) at the University of Illinois may be used to illustrate this research. Five parallel programmes were introduced to classes of pre-school children. These are described by Karnes as:

Traditional — in which the children were encouraged to follow their own interests, and the staff instructed to take advantage of opportunities for informally stimulating the children's interest, questioning and encouraging them to talk.

Community integrated — which was very similar to the traditional but in which social integration was encouraged between the few disadvantaged children and the majority of middle- and upper-class children.

Montessori — was a carefully designed programme of structured activities, though without the teacher playing a direct instructional role.

Karnes Structured Cognitive — used short small group sessions in which the teacher utilized the resources of concrete materials and games to encourage the children to verbalize their understanding of situations. The emphasis was on improving children's ability, but in a meaningful context.

Bereiter-Englemann — used intensive oral drill in verbal and logical patterns. Learning a pattern by rote was followed by generalization to new situations.

These five programmes were defined as on a dimension increasing 'structure'.

The results after one year were quite clear. On measures of cognitive and verbal ability, children who had experienced the 'Bereiter-Englemann' and 'Karnes Structured Cognitive' programmes showed the greatest improvement, followed by the 'Traditional' nursery programme. Least successful were the 'Montessori' and 'Community Integrated' programmes. The finding is interpreted by Karnes as indicating that if a programme is to be successful it must be closely structured. The only exception is the apparent 'failure' of the Montessori structured programme, which suggests that what is important for the success of the programme is not simply the degree of structure; more critical is the extent of meaningful adult-child verbal interaction.

Explanations for programme effectiveness

The evaluations we have described all appear to demonstrate that the most effective way of improving children's verbal abilities through nursery education is by providing a closely structured programme incorporating intensive adult-child instructional contact. But before drawing firm conclusions on this issue it will be wise to examine in a little more detail possible alternative interpretations of the result.

Without doubt, the results are to some degree an artefact of the design and methods of the evaluations. By comparison with informal methods, structured programmes have characteristics which render them much more readily amenable to evaluation by traditional experimental methods. In a number of important respects, the content and presentation of the structured programmes corresponded to the design of the evaluation.

Firstly, the circumstances in which the structured programmes and the assessments were administered were quite similar. Each required the child to co-operate in a one-to-one or small group relationship with an adult, to sustain concentration on a task prescribed by the adult and follow detailed instructions. It is possible that the successful programmes are so partly because they teach the child how to respond to an instructional/test situation, rather than actually improving their verbal ability. Indeed there is good evidence that low scores of disadvantaged children on intelligence tests may be due to their unfamilarity with the demands of the test situation (Hertzig, Birch *et al.*, 1968; Zigler and Butterfield, 1968), a problem which might well be overcome by an intensive structured programme.

The possibility that the dramatic success of these programmes is the result of improving children's command of the test situation is further supported by the evidence from the NFER evaluation that length of experience is not closely related to programme effectiveness. This is contrary to the expectation that a programme designed to provide a continuous and developing educational experience would produce continuing improvements, and suggests that the initial 'boost' observed may represent a fairly superficial change in performance and not a fundamental improvement in verbal ability.

The present studies cannot entirely resolve this issue. It is very probable that children who are not familiar with the didactic nature of the test situation will find it less easy to cope with than those who have experienced the didactic approach of a structured programme, but this is not the sole explanation for children's improvements.

There is good evidence that a major part of the effectiveness of a structured programme is accounted for by its specific content. It will be recalled that the Birmingham Number Programme which was compared with the Peabody Kit was didactic and quite similar in teaching method, but the technique relied heavily on non-verbal methods of instruction, and of course the aim was not primarily to develop children's verbal abilities. The comparison of the Number Programme with Peabody groups demonstrated that the effectiveness of the programme was not solely due to increased familiarity with the intensive instructional situation; although the children made gains on the language tests these were not as great as those made by their peers who had experienced Peabody.

However, although this study controlled for the similar style of presentation of the programme and the tests, there are other factors which may be responsible for the greater success of structured programmes and could not be controlled for in any of the studies.

The skills taught by the Peabody Kit were verbal skills of a particular kind, taught in a particular way and relying heavily on "artificial" language games. These are the very same type of skills tested by the assessment instruments used. Arguably a more valid measure of children's improvement as a result of informal programmes would require comparable informal assessment methods. Such methods would assess children's competence in using language in a more natural learning situation. Courtney Cazden has coined the terms 'contrived encounters' versus 'concentrated encounters' to describe the differences between the two approaches to assessment (Cazden, forthcoming). There are very grave difficulties involved in developing assessment techniques which are informal but also reliable; hence the reliance of the research projects on well-tried psychometric techniques. Nevertheless, unless such techniques are employed it is arguable that we cannot make a valid evaluation of informal methods.

The final point of correspondence between the design of the structured programmes and evaluations relates to the high level of control demanded by each. The programmes exclusively teach a series of specific language objectives, and the assessment instruments exclusively measure a similar series of objectives. By contrast an informal programme teaches language objectives within the context of a much broader set of objectives, and the learning outcomes of the programme are accordingly more diffuse.

The significance to the 'success' of a project of ensuring correspondence between the style of the programme and the evaluation may be clarified by reference to the problems faced by research teams who did try to evaluate the more informal programmes.

By choosing to work with an informal nursery programme, these projects sacrificed ease of evaluation for acceptability and relevance to the teachers and children. The conflict between these two goals is illustrated by the Deptford team. Early attempts to formalize and specify some aspects of the content of the nursery programme were met with the objection from teachers that they were not being involved sufficiently in the design of the programme, that the setting was artificial and the programme did not allow sufficiently for working from the spontaneous interests of the child. The teachers' argument for spontaneity implied that the programme should consist of a range of possiblities, that although there would be some consistency in teachers' pattern of response to an activity, there would also be an element of uncertainty. By contrast the tradtional research methods available to the team endeavour to reduce uncertainty to a minimum, in this case to define the teaching objectives and methods which are to be studied, concentrate on the influence of these on the children, and eliminate or control other extraneous influences. Having chosen to work within a different model of teaching in the nursery, the Deptford and Dundee research teams both recognized the inappropriateness of conventional research techniques and were forced to seek alternative techniques which would enable a more valid assessment to be made of the informal nursery programme.

The Deptford team offer the most interesting alternative evaluation technique, which depended on making observations of the different educational treatments received by children in the experimental and control groups. The team developed their own Nursery Class Observation Schedule, based on American work by Medley *et al.*, (1968). The schedule used time-sampling techniques to observe the context and character of interactions between children and adults (teachers and nursery assistants) in the experimental and control nursery classes.

The analysis of these recordings indicated that the staff of the experimental classes were more often available to interact with the children than in the control classes. Moreover, the introduction of the programme appeared to have caused a shift in the role-differentiation of teachers and assistants. In the "control" groups their roles appeared to be similar, whereas in the "programme" groups the teachers interacted with the children a great deal more than the assistants. However, although the overall number of interactions in the "programme" groups was greater, the ratio of interactions intended to convey information to those concerned with procedural matters did not vary. It seems that although the staff were taking greater care to engage the children in conversation, they were perhaps lacking sufficient skill to make the conversation serve an educational function.

This departure from traditional methods of collecting data in an evaluation has the advantage not only of showing whether a programme is being effective, but also of indicating what may be its limitations. This contrasts with pre-test/post-test comparisons which make clear whether a programme has succeeded or failed on specific criteria but does not provide any information as to why. Observational techniques of evaluation are increasingly being used in educational research to supplement more conventional psychometric methods. They will be discussed further in the next chapter.

Conclusion

In conclusion, we should not assume that because the conventional nursery programme does not produce striking gains on tests of verbal ability, it should be replaced by more formal methods. Before jumping to a hasty conclusion it is advisable that the adequacy of our research methods be examined and more appropriate methods employed in future evaluations.

At the same time the potential of the more structured methods has been established. They can be used to improve the performance of children significantly by the end of their nursery experience. But whether or not such methods are introduced in nursery education will depend on numerous factors besides the simple effectiveness of the method.

Firstly, there is no one criterion of effectiveness, even in promoting language development. As we have seen different programmes have different effects; the Peabody is particularly valuable in promoting children's knowledge of vocabulary, the Individual Programme seemed to improve knowledge of grammatical structure (page 57). Secondly there is disagreement over whether it is desirable to pay such concentrated attention to one aspect of children's development, possibly to the detriment of other aspects. Nursery education has always had much broader objectives than encouraging language development, yet most of the comparisons between the special programmes and normal nursery education have only taken these as criteria. To evaluate the traditional programme solely on these grounds is analagous to testing a vehicle for speed when it has been designed for economy. More adequate evaluation of programmes with broader objectives must clearly take account of the full spectrum of functions in children's development.

Thirdly, all too often the structured programme is associated with the formality, inflexibility, and prescribed nature of a kit like Peabody. It is unlikely that these are the qualities which account for the Kit's effectiveness. The fact that the most effective programmes all employ intensive adult-child verbal interaction as their key educational strategy points to this as the critical feature in their success rather than their superficial formality. This educational strategy could be put into practice through a formalized programme of lessons or through the nursery teacher and assistant devising their own programme to optimize planned intervention in children's activities.

In the last analysis, it is probably more important that staff should be committed and enthusiastic about the educational programme they are providing than that they follow any particular proven method. A comparative study by Weikart (1972) confirms this interpretation. Careful training and preparation ensured that staff morale and involvement in the administration of all the programmes in his study were optimized. In this study no differences were found in the effectiveness of the various programmes.

Finally the choice of programme is not just a question of which is the most effective, but which is most compatible to the aims and circumstances of the nursery. In some cases children's attainments as a result of the programme may play a small part in deciding its appropriateness. Although the compensatory model tends to assume educational attainment is the most important goal, this was not universally adhered to even by the EPA teams. In particular, 'Dr. Wotever' developed by the Liverpool team was designed to reflect the experiences of the child. This was the overriding goal, improvements in attainment taking secondary place.

The other factor affecting the use of special programmes is likely to be the circumstances of the nursery and the training of the staff. In the section describing the main evaluation of the Peabody Kit it was noted that there were inconsistencies in the size of improvements made by children as a result of their experience of the Kit (page 47). In general, the greatest improvements were made by children attending nurseries with the least adequate educational facilities. In the better equipped nurseries, staff may have possessed the skills which enabled them to achieve the objectives of Peabody but within the context of an informal nursery programme.

There can be no universal prescription for a pre-school programme. A formal programme like the Peabody Kit may be a great deal more suitable to a playgroup which lacks equipment and qualified staff, and also to nurseries which may already provide an excellent programme but have not traditionally placed great emphasis on language skills. For these groups use of the programme might provide a valuable induction into teaching language skills, although in the long term it seems probable that a kit may best be used as a resource to be drawn upon rather than a programme to be followed.

(3) The long-term effects of special programmes

Previous sections have established the considerable potential of using various types of educational experience to boost the language performance of pre-school children. Unfortunately, this alone has not always been considered sufficient evidence of the merits of nursery experience. A higher expectation for the potential of nursery education has been created than for any other stage of education.

This is one sector of education which is not compulsory. Perhaps this partly accounts for the expectation that nursery education should be able to prove itself not only as providing a valuable educational experience for pre-school children, but as having impact on the children's educational progress long after they have left the nursery for compulsory schooling. Responsibility also lies with the advocates of nursery education who have sometimes made exaggerated claims on its behalf. Researchers too have played their part, interpreting the theory that the early years are the formative period in the child's development as implying that appropriate intervention at this age will have a major effect on the children's subsequent progress. Irrespective of the merits of the argument, the consequence has been that when nursery programmes have been evaluated, the criterion has tended to be their long-term effects. Consequently the 'success' of intervention programmes has largely stood or fallen by their ability to demonstrate long-term effects. (See, for example, Tizard, B., 1975, p. 4.)

Of the projects we have described, in only two were the nursery children followed-up to assess their subsequent progress in primary school. These were the NFER and the West Riding EPA projects.

The children in the NFER project were followed-up through two stages of infant schooling. The team considered that the most crucial test of the effectiveness of a programme would be the ability of children to transfer the skills taught into the new school situation. They chose to assess the children soon after they could be expected to have 'settled-in' to the new atmosphere. A verbal ability measure, the Boehm Test of Basic Concepts (Boehm, 1969) was administered during the second half of the children's first term in the infant school. At the same time teachers were asked to complete an Adjustment to School Scale (Thompson, 1975) which might indicate any differences between the groups in terms of ease of transition to the new school. The second stage of the follow-up was at the end of the children's sixth term (second year) in infants' school, when the children were administered a test of Reading (Gates MacGinitie Test, 1972) and Maths (Basic Maths Test, ETS, 1966). At the same time teachers were asked to complete two scales measuring children's classroom behaviour and adjustment (Hess, 1966; Rutter, 1967). The team faced serious problems of tracing all the children who had dispersed to 21 schools within Slough, as well as numerous others outside the Borough. Nevertheless, of the original 272 children for whom complete data were available from the nursery phase, 180 were successfully followed-up.

The results at the first stage of follow-up illustrate how quickly the advantage of one group over another may be dissipated. The test of verbal ability was administered only three months after post-testing had shown the clear advantage of the Peabody group on the criterion measures, and yet there was now no significant difference, merely a slight trend favouring this group. No differences were apparent on the measure of adjustment to school. The pattern of results was repeated at the second stage of follow-up with no differences on the measures of classroom behaviour or reading and maths. Any advantage of the Peabody group had disappeared on these attainment tests by the age of seven. Furthermore, a comparison with other children in the infant schools revealed no advantage of either of the nursery groups, 'programme' or 'normal nursery' over 'other nursery' or 'direct entry groups'.

These results do not offer much support for the argument that early education can make children better prepared for school. The special programme does not appear to have had any impact on the children's ability to master the skills of reading. At best the programme has had a short-term effect on the specific abilities it set out to teach.

Some additional light is thrown on these findings by the West Riding follow-up which adopted a slightly different design and other criteria of long-term success. The children were followed up in two primary schools at the end of their first, second and third years. By the end of the reception year the performance of all three groups (Peabody, Individual and Normal programmes) had converged to produce similar scores on the EPVT and Reynell Developmental Language Scale. Apparently the effect of a common infant school experience had been to 'wash-out' the differential effects of the various nursery school programmes.

However, an additional analysis of the West Riding data is possible. Since the team used the same standardized measure of verbal ability at both nursery and follow-up stages, it is possible to examine whether the gains made as a result of nursery experience have been maintained into the infant school. The results showed that children not only maintained the gains they had made by the end of the nursery phase; they also continued to improve during the reception class. This might be interpreted as merely due to increased test familiarity. It was, after all, the third time children had been administered the same tests. However the results of the subsequent follow-up rule out this explanation. The increased scores at the end of the reception class year turned out to be the peak of the nursery children's performance, which had declined by the second and third year, whereas a test-familiarity effect would have predicted that the improvement would continue.

It must be emphasized at this point that when the words 'improve', 'gain', 'decline' or 'deteriorate' are used in relation to children's scores on standardized tests, the meaning is quite specific. The terms do not refer directly to improvements or deteriorations in a child's ability. Generally speaking they refer to the rate at which a child's abilities are developing by comparison with other children in the same age-group. Hence if a group of children have improved their average score this indicates that they have been developing at a faster rate than they were. A group whose average score has declined have not ceased to develop, nor have they regressed, but they are now learning at a slower rate than they were.

To return to the West Riding follow-up data, there appear to be two possible explanations for the continued improvement of the ex-nursery children. It can be interpreted as evidence of the long-term benefits of nursery school attendance, whatever the programme. Alternatively, the convergence of scores suggests that the improvement may result from the educational experiences provided in the reception class. In fact both of these provide a partial explanation.

The West Riding team were able to make comparisons with an earlier survey of all children (including non-nursery attenders) during their first three years in primary school. The results of this survey show a similar peak-performance at the end of the children's first year. Clearly, then, the reception class is having a booster-effect on all children, which may account for the continued gains by the ex-nursery children. At the same time this comparison shows that overall the ex-nursery children were performing at a considerably higher level at all stages of the investigation, which points to a long-term effect of nursery education.

To summarize these follow-up studies: in one respect the results of the NFER and EPA evaluation are consistent. In both cases the differences in score between programme and comparison groups disappeared, which is evidence that the beneficial effects of a special programme were not sustained through the infant school. But in another respect the results differ. The NFER team found no differences between either ex-nursery groups and a direct-entry group, whereas the EPA team found a clear advantage of the ex-nursery groups.

Reconciliation of this discrepancy may lie in the type of assessments used in the follow-up. Unlike the West Riding team, NFER did not use the same instruments in the follow-up as had been used in the nursery stage. Consequently for the nursery groups to show an advantage over direct-entry groups would have required not only that they continue to show improved verbal performance but that the skills learned in nursery had equipped them better to master reading and maths. Exclusive reliance by NFER on these criteria of the long-term effectiveness of the nursery programme betrays what was perhaps an over-ambitious faith in the potential of early intervention. It is too much to expect of an early education programme that it alone can fundamentally alter children's later learning. In America, after the 'failure' of early Headstart programmes, a number of projects have been set up to examine whether pre-school programmes can have long-term benefits if they are followed through by appropriate reinforcement in later education. The results of these projects have been quite promising (Bissell, 1973).

A similar follow-through was conducted on a small scale by the West

Riding team in one of the infant schools to which children in the nursery experiment had transferred. The intake was divided into two groups, one of which experienced an individual programme designed to follow-on from nursery work and administered with the assistance of students on teaching-practice. When the children were retested at the end of their reception class year the children who had experienced the follow-through programme obtained significantly higher scores on the EPVT and the Comprehension Scale of the RDLS.

Although the follow-through programme did not continue, these children were followed-up on the same measures for the subsequent two years. The same pattern of converging scores was repeated so that within two years the programme group showed no advantage on any of the measures (Smith and James, 1975, p. 234). Clearly, while the children's earlier learning is being reinforced and developed the advantage of the programme groups is maintained. However as soon as the support is withdrawn the children's performance will tend to revert to its initial level. It seems that intervention may be effective in the infant as well as the nursery school. But to be truly effective it must be sustained throughout schooling.

Conclusion

Interpretation of these results has been rather complicated; it is to be hoped that the discussion has demonstrated how difficult it is to make an adequate evaluation of an early education programme.

Barbara Tizard has recently reminded us that: 'A child who attends a half-day nursery school from his third to his fifth birthday will have spent only about four per cent of the waking hours of the first five years of his life at school' (Tizard, 1975, p. 8). We must not expect too much from nursery education, however intensive the programme. In future it would be advisable if greater realism were to be shown by all, including those who have been too optimistic about the potential of early intervention and those who may be tempted to. use evidence of apparent long-term 'failure' as justification for withdrawing support for nursery education.

The early years are certainly the formative years, during which the child is acquiring basic skills which will be the foundation for later learning. The single piece of research most often quoted in this respect is the review of longitudinal studies by Bloom (1964) from which it is concluded that children's intelligence on leaving school can largely be predicted when they have barely begun it. Inequalities are established early in life, when the child is most susceptible to the influence of the environment. Hence the conclusion that the first five years are the most important, that this is the time when education can most profitably intervene.

Unfortunately those who have eagerly clutched this evidence of the value of early education have all too often failed to recognize its other implication. Just as the early years are the time when the progress of the child's development may most readily be boosted, they are also the time when the child is most susceptible to the effects of adverse circumstances. The very malleability of the child at this age means that skills quickly acquired may just as quickly be lost. There are numerous other influences on the child besides the nursery which may not serve to consolidate and reinforce what the child has learned. The child entering primary school at five is only a little less vulnerable and suggestible than when he entered the nursery at three and may easily be adversely affected by any discontinuities associated with the transition. In conclusion, while nursery education continues to be viewed as a cure for social ills and inequalities, it is unlikely to prosper. Research has been partly responsible for the creation, and also for the destruction of this myth. The sooner nursery education is viewed as an integral part of the continuous process of education, serving an immediate as well as a long-term purpose, and evaluated on these terms, the better. A shift in the emphasis of research is beginning to take place. Some of this will be reported in the next chapter.

Chapter V

Innovation and evaluation in nursery education

The purpose of this chapter is to describe some of the promising lines of development in research which have taken place since the projects we have been discussing were commissioned. Changes may be observed in both the 'action' and the 'research' elements of recent projects.

Innovation in nursery education

One of the goals of the EPA and NFER research was to demonstrate the possibility of using pre-school education as an instrument of positive discrimination to reduce educational disadvantage and social inequalities. As such the research was an experiment in social engineering which used nursery education as the technology. With the emphasis on producing improvements in children's ability, relatively less emphasis was placed on the development of programmes specially designed to suit the circumstances of the nurseries involved.

Consequently, although the research was able to demonstrate that by using special programmes it is possible to make substantial improvements in children's abilities, at least in the short term, the practical feasibility and desirability of attempting to do so on a large scale by these methods is open to doubt. However impressed the researchers may be by their relative success in producing significant short-term gains in children's ability as a result of introducing special programmes like the Peabody, teachers are not likely to be greatly influenced when the character of the special programme is so markedly different from the educational climate currently found in most nurseries. This is evidenced by the relatively small number of nurseries which appear to be making use of such programmes.

The strategy adopted by the research teams suited their purpose of demonstrating the possibility of compensatory education; to make compensatory education a part of the daily curriculum of all nurseries requires a different approach. To be successful the programme must arise from, and be fully integrated within the traditional nursery day. Since the traditional programme is not formally prescribed, but arises out of the individual teacher's skill in making use of situations as they arise, any changes must be made in conjunction with teachers. They will result from altering the teacher's perception of children's development and the practices which are appropriate.

Some of the programmes developed by the EPA teams as alternatives to Peabody illustrate this approach, for example in Deptford and Dundee. But these attempts at curriculum development were exploratory and localized in a small group of nurseries. Wider dissemination of new ideas and improved nursery practices requires a project conducted at a national level. Two examples currently underway are concerned with early mathematical experiences (by Professor and Mrs Mathews at Chelsea College) and children's learning style (by NFER). The project which has aroused the greatest interest and, although not yet complete, seems likely to be the most successful in terms of its influence on nursery practices nationwide is being sponsored by Schools Council and directed by Dr Joan Tough.

Dr Tough has rejected approaches to the disadvantaged child which treat him as requiring a separate structured programme like the ones we have been discussing (Tough, forthcoming a). Her own approach is to focus on one part of the nursery programme, the adult-child dialogue, and her method is to encourage the teacher to develop an understanding of the potential within this dialogue for fostering children's language and thinking. The adult-child dialogue is also the essence of the teaching method used by the structured programmes, but Dr Tough advocates that to be successful it must be used flexibly by the teacher who is sensitive to the character of the children with whom she is working. Consequently Dr Tough always works closely with the teachers who must put into practice the teaching techniques developed.

Entitled *Communication Skills in Early Childhood*, the strategy of the project has been to convene working groups of teachers, located throughout the country. Dr Tough called for the participation of teachers in these working groups in the newsheet of the Schools Council and described their function and relation to the research team:

'On the one hand the team will be putting forward ideas and asking for the teachers' views on these; they will also ask teachers to try out particular strategies and to record the children's responses. On the other hand, the working parties will also be generating ideas from their accumulated experience, trying these themselves, and then submitting them for consideration to other working parties.'

(Tough, 1973a)

The purposes and design of the research are not the only features which mark it off as distinct from most of the studies we have discussed. An additional characteristic of the approach is its foundation in a radically different model of the language of disadvantaged children, a model which prescribes quite different methods of remediation.

This alternative model results from the considerable advances which have been made in research on the differences in verbal ability between social groups since the EPA and NFER projects were conceived. The most influential theory on the formulation of intervention strategies in these projects was that of 'restricted' and 'elaborated' language codes. Briefly summarized the theory argued that mastery of language is the key to success in school, and that differences in language ability between social classes arise out of their social circumstances and life styles. The difference between the restricted and the elaborated codes was described primarily in terms of structural aspects of speech, namely children's grammatical competence and vocabulary. Accordingly the intervention programmes concentrated on training children in competence in use of the structural possibilities in language.

Subsequently a number of studies began to throw doubt on the generality of the restricted/elaborated code hypothesis. Apparently, although the speech of groups of working class children could generally be described as restricted, in certain contexts they were quite capable of producing elaborated speech, e.g. formal versus informal letter writing (Lawton, 1963) and speech when probed by a questioner (Williams and Naremore, 1969a).

Such conclusions were given further support by the work of William Labov with children in Harlem. Labov (1969) argued that in the typical child-adult/teacher/researcher relationship, these children might be perceived as near mute. Yet in a less threatening situation, sitting around on the floor eating potato crisps, these children show evidence of a structurally elaborate language. Apparently social context is a most important determinant of speech code. In the face of these apparent complexities to the theory of social differences in speech codes, a number of theorists have shifted the emphasis of their discussions away from structural differences and towards differences in language usage by different social groups (see paper by Halliday, 1973; Williams and Naremore, 1969b; developed further by Halliday, 1975; and applied to the classroom by Cazden, John and Hymes, 1972).

In an earlier study, *The Pre-School Language Project*, Joan Tough (1973; forthcoming b) has been responsible for collecting evidence on British children to support the argument that more important than children's grammatical competence is their willingness to use language to express themselves, and the specific functions to which they put it. This research compared 24 children from social class I with 24 from social classes IV and V at ages three, five-and-a-half, and seven-and-a-half. Recording children's speech in situations of play and interaction with a peer, the speech of the two groups was found to differ both in structure and function. The speech of advantaged children showed longer mean length of utterance (MLU), greater noun phrase and verb phrase complexity, and higher frequency of pronoun use.

However Tough argues (forthcoming a) that unless these differences in structural complexity reflect variations in the quality of meaning expressed, there is no reason why such differences should of themselves have educational significance. An analysis of the functions for which the children used language reveals that they do indeed show expected differences. Although all children used language for the maintainance of status, rights and property, as well as to issue threats and criticism, the advantaged children showed a much higher incidence of using speech for recall, association, analysis of details, synthesis, anticipation, prediction, collaboration and planning, giving explanations, projecting through imagination and making hypotheses.

It would be misleading to imply that evidence of the importance of social class differences in language usage is entirely new. Within Bernstein's own papers there is a considerable amount of discussion of their functional origins. He argued that restricted code is primarily concerned with the maintainance of status and solidarity; the language used is contextually dependent. By contrast, elaborated code is used to explore social relations and requires articulating meanings independent of social context. However the search for evidence for the theory has always tended to focus on the realization of different functions in the structural qualities of speech. This probably reflected the enormous impact of Chomsky's structural linguistic theory of transformational grammar on the social sciences in the sixties.

The real importance of the shift in emphasis towards differences in the functions for which children use language is the implications for the appropriate teaching methods for disadvantaged children. Joan Tough argues that it may be most productive to devise strategies encouraging children to develop different uses of language. She argues that it is artificial and inefficient to use drill methods to teach grammar, and her view is supported by several other researches (e.g. Cazden, 1965; Moffett, 1968), and is reiterated in the recent report of the Bullock Committee (DES 1975b, Chap. 5.). Her own approach is to encourage teachers to make accurate assessments of children's verbal competence (without using formal tests of any kind) and intervene in children's activities informally as opportunities present themselves.

The wheel has turned full circle. The early compensatory programmes arose out of dissatisfaction with traditional nursery methods to help disadvantaged children master language. Now that the theory of the language of disadvantaged children has changed, suddenly these methods appear to be the appropriate ones. All that seems to be required is to provide guidance for teachers to ensure that they make full use of the opportunities afforded by the nursery for promotion of the language abilities of all their children.

Problems of informal methods

Although informal methods will no doubt provide the model for future development in nursery education, there are certain inherent dangers which must be guarded against, particularly if nursery education is to fulfil its obligation to disadvantaged children. Informal methods are very easily open to misuse. They make special demands on the child's ability to take full advantage of activities provided, and correspondingly special demands are made on the teacher to ensure that each child is gaining the maximum benefit from the activities.

The great advantage of a formal approach like the Peabody Kit is that the choice of activities, their presentation, and their sequencing are controlled by the teacher. The 'structure' of learning is explicit in a formal programme, whereas in the informal nursery, the structure is intrinsic to the total situation, particularly the relationships between the child, the activities and the teacher. Accordingly, the organization of learning is as much controlled by the child as by the teacher. It is assumed that the child has a natural curiosity and by following his own interests will obtain a balanced diet; that he will know how to pursue an activity to gain the maximum benefit from it; that he will be able to transfer the skill learned in one activity to a new situation; and that he will progress in his learning from simple to more complex skills.

Such an approach tends to disregard the possibility that there may be some disadvantaged children whose 'natural' curiosity has been suppressed, and whose 'interests' are not closely tied to educational goals. For such children active intervention by the teacher may be required.

Joan Tough argues that the teacher can work successfully in the informal situation to foster the children's development. In the following instance the emphasis is on language:

> 'By paying attention to one child's talking for a few minutes on several occasions the teacher can learn about the child's difficulties and can hold them in mind and find ways of helping him as opportunities arise naturally during the day.'
>
> (Tough 1973b, p. 61)

Let us examine in a little more detail the implications of this approach for the demands which will be made on the teacher. These will certainly include the following: She must pay particular attention to which activities each child is following, and offer guidance in the selection of other activities which are being neglected. She must identify and give special help to the child who may show impulsiveness in his choice of activities, lack concentration and perseverance and be easily distracted to a more 'attractive' activity, or one which his friends are pursuing. Finally she must ensure that the child's use of activities is developing constructively and not remaining static; the teacher may need to provide a new stimulus to challenge the child's understanding.

These dangers are all 'taken-care of', in a prescribed programme, which is carefully designed to be systematic, to develop consistent themes, to provide continuity between activities, and continually present the child with new challenges which discourage stagnation and encourage progression. Intensive interaction with a small group of children also sensitizes the teacher to any particular difficulties being experienced by the children. The success of informal methods depends on the ability of the teacher to maintain *implicity* in the quality of her organization of activities and interaction with children, the structure, sequence and control which is maintained *explicitly* in a formal programme.

The main source of the dangers in the informal learning situation lies in the commitment to 'individual learning'. Success depends very largely on the teacher's ability to assess the progress of each individual child separately, to know his strengths and weaknesses and to design a programme accordingly. The teacher must possess great resourcefulness to know how to make the best use of situations which arise and opportunities for development which are presented in the children's play activities.

Of critical importance is the teacher's capacity to monitor her own behaviour, to keep record of which children she has spent time with, and for what purpose, in order to ensure that her time is profitably used, and evenly distributed amongst the children who would benefit from it. The danger is that a large amount of the teacher's time may be spent dealing with routine matters, and that the remainder may be concentrated on the children who are most demanding, those who are most persistent in their requests for the teacher's attention, and those whom the teacher feels most able to help. In this situation, where the teacher may lose full control over how she spends her time, it is very easy for some children to be neglected; and in some cases the children who 'miss-out' may be those who would most benefit from the teacher's time, notably the shy or withdrawn. At worst, where there are inequalities in teacher-child contact, the so-called 'Pygmalion-effect' might even develop (Rosenthal and Jacobson, 1968).

In these circumstances a vicious circle is set-up — teacher's low expectations for a child are transmitted to him through her 'negative' behaviour. It is suggested that the child perceives the low expectations of the teacher and his behaviour in turn confirms the teacher's expectations. This teacher-learner cycle of expectations and behaviour is certainly present in every learning situation. Indeed it is the expressed intention of teachers to use it in quite the opposite way from this; they intend that their behaviour should transmit positive encouragement to the children who are perceived as needing most help. The teacher's success in this respect will depend entirely on her ability to diagnose correctly the requirements of the individual child and her capacity to monitor and control her attention accordingly, to ensure that it is appropriate and distributed amongst all children, including those who need it as well as those who demand it.

The evidence for the 'Pygmalion effect' is controversial. Nevertheless, the dangers associated with the teacher's attempts to distribute attention between children are clear, and the operation of the Pygmalion process has been described in American primary classrooms, by Brophy and Good (1970).

These issues are particularly applicable to all informal learning situations and they are currently being discussed with reference to modern trends towards 'open' primary education, for example Boydell (1975a) and Tough (1975). These criticisms should not be construed by the reader as indicative that the author's own preference is for structured programmes. The purpose of highlighting the possible dangers inherent in informal methods is as an introduction to the question of how they may most usefully be evaluated to ensure that these problems do not arise. It is to this question that we now turn.

Evaluation of the informal nursery programme

The EPA and NFER projects relied almost exclusively on use of psychometric methods in the evaluation of the programmes they developed and introduced. Assessments which reflected the teaching objectives of the programmes were selected and administered to children before and after nursery experience. These methods were ideally suited to evaluating a prescribed programme with a clearly defined and quite narrow set of objectives, but as the Deptford EPA team found, were quite unsuited to the more diffuse goals of the informal nursery programme (see page 61 for discussion). Psychometric methods cannot capture the wealth of potential benefits afforded by the informal regime. Development of assessment methods which are suited to the goals of nursery education and may be administered by teachers is the task of a current NFER project.

To make a complete evaluation of the quality of the learning situation in the nursery requires a different approach altogether. The method tried out by the Deptford EPA team was to carry out structured observations of the staff and children in the nursery. This has the advantage of enabling the research to make an assessment of the quality of the educational environment and the resultant children's play. It is also ideally suited to throwing light on the potential problems of informal education which we have been discussing. The technique has been used successfully by a few recent studies which highlight the character of teaching strategies in British primary classrooms, for example (Resnick, 1972; Garner and Bing, 1973; Boydell, 1975b). There are also two studies to report which have specifically examined nursery education. The first is a small-scale study by Valerie Thomas (1973), whose main focus was on the quality of the children's language in response to the educational environment provided by the staff. Children and staff in three nursery classes were studied. Thomas found a general paucity of adult speech serving a specifically educational function. Staff speech to the children was mostly concerned with their care function, and their utterances did not appear to be adapted to children's ability level.

Barbara Tizard, Janet Philps and Ian Plewis (1975) have conducted an observational study which examines the issues raised by Valerie Thomas in more depth. Their study of 12 nurseries describes the quality of the educational environment provided by the staff. To achieve this a systematic observation procedure was adapted from that used in earlier studies of residential homes for young children (Tizard *et al.*, 1972). The procedure consisted of observing staff behaviour in terms of a number of relevant pre-defined categories which included both what the adult said to and what she did for the children in her care. By way of illustration three of the categories used by Tizard were:

> '"Questions child for information, or gives child simple information or opinions."
> "Affection, i.e. gives physical comfort, sits child on knee, puts arm round child, etc."
> "Instructs, i.e. verbally explains to child how to carry out task".'
> (taken from Tizard *et al.*, 1975, Table 2)

Each category was assigned a number. The task of the observer was to note the categories as they occurred using a time-sampling method (in this case noting all the categories which describe events for the first five seconds of every thirty seconds).

The picture which was obtained by these methods was of staff who were actively supervising children's activity, but were not observed to engage frequently in direct instruction. The behaviours which were observed most frequently were 'questions and gives simple information' (in 18.6 per cent of observations), 'deals with play equipment' (16.5 per cent) and minimal supervision (13.5 per cent). The activities least frequently observed were those which, for example, involved the teacher questioning a child to help him solve a problem, demonstrating a skill, or suggesting ways a child might extend an activity. These all occurred in less than one per cent of observations.

In addition to this overall description of staff behaviour, Tizard was able to examine the way staff behaviour varied according to the type of children in the nurseries. The 12 nurseries were divided into two groups: six catered for a majority of children whose fathers pursued 'Professional' or 'Managerial' occupations (the middle class nurseries); the other six catered mostly for children whose fathers were manual workers (the working class nurseries). When the nurseries were compared in this way consistent differences were found. The more instructional types of staff behaviour were observed much more frequently in the middle class centres. These included 'gives and asks for simple information', 'reads aloud', 'makes simple suggestions'. The total 'teacher-talk' was also much higher in these nurseries. By contrast the categories observed more often in the working class centres were 'minimal supervision' and 'deals with play equipment'.

These results certainly seem to confirm some of the fears expressed earlier about the skill of nursery staff in using informal nursery teaching methods. It appears that the general 'cognitive' content of the nursery programme is quite low, and that it is especially low in the nurseries catering for children who might most benefit from opportunities to develop intellectual and language skills.

There are several possible explanations for these effects. The differences between the nurseries may be due to the different expectations of the staff for the children based on knowledge of their home backgrounds. But more probably, perhaps, the 'atmosphere' in the two types of nursery may have reflected the attitudes, interests and stage of development of the children themselves. The staff in the 'middle class' centres may have been responding to the verbally articulate, inquisitive and cognitively-orientated children in their care. This would be supported by the genuine differences in performance on the Reynell Developmental Language Scale which Tizard reports. But on the other hand she also states that observations of the children in the nurseries did not reveal any differences in the frequency with which middle class and working class children approached the staff. Clarification of the 'issue' will have to await further analysis of these data and other studies of similar issues which are at present underway (e.g. by Asher Cashdan and Janet Philps at the Open University, and Corinne Hutt at Keele University).

Whatever the explanation, these results present a depressing picture.

However, a further analysis conducted by Barbara Tizard also suggests possible measures which might be taken to improve the quality of the nursery educational environment in the nursery.

The 12 nurseries in her study were not all of the same type. They were roughly comparable in terms of superficial qualities such as size, staffing ratios, resources and equipment, but differed considerably in terms of their educational orientation. There were three groups: the first group of four 'low educational orientation' nurseries were generally playgroups or private nurseries where the staff were not trained teachers (Tizard denotes these 'E—' nurseries); the middle group of three consisted of ordinary nursery schools following a conventional programme ('E' nurseries); the final group of four were nursery schools which basically followed a conventional programme but also incorporated some special cognitive content ('E+' nurseries). In each group, two were 'middle class' and two were 'working class' nurseries, in accordance with the design of the analysis previously discussed. The two 'working class' 'E+' nurseries were in fact nursery schools which had been involved in the NFER evaluation of Peabody which had been completed one year earlier.

With this design, Tizard was able to compare the educational quality and the children's abilities in nurseries with varying educational orientations, with very interesting results. Not surprisingly staff in the 'E—' nurseries spent more time supervising the children and much less time actively instructing them than in the 'E' and 'E+' nurseries. But there were also marked differences between the two types of nursery school. Much less time was spent in supervision in the 'E+' schools and much more time giving and asking for simple information. Tizard reports that the cognitive content of staff behaviour in the 'E+ working class' nurseries was higher than in the 'E' middle class nurseries although there were still social class differences within 'E+' nursery schools. The test scores of the children follow a similar pattern.

Clearly the decision by the 'E+' nurseries to incorporate a cognitive element in the programme has had a beneficial effect on the quality of educational experience provided for the children. The results are particularly encouraging for the two 'E+' centres which had been involved in the NFER evaluation. Although neither of the nursery schools had continued to make formal use of the Peabody Kit, nevertheless the long-term effects of using the Kit are quite clear.

Perhaps the greatest impact of introducing a special programme into nurseries has not been on the small number of children involved in the EPA and NFER evaluations but on the large number of children who will benefit over the years from the enhanced quality of the educational environment now provided by the staff of those nurseries. Indeed the programme is likely to have improved for these children by virtue of now being integrated within the nursery day rather than separated off and taught as a special session. Whereas formerly the Peabody teacher could not always make use of the opportunities throughout the day to reinforce the concepts and skills taught by the programme, now the teacher can make systematic use of a variety of situations and circumstances as opportunities for using diverse methods to achieve educational objectives.

The possible value of providing a prescribed set of language and intellectual activities as a tool for training staff has been mentioned already (page 63). It is not intended that this should substitute for the more insightful methods advocated by Joan Tough. Through discussion and examples, many teachers are helped to make more precise assessments of children's verbal abilities and to provide an 'enabling' curriculum in which these may be fostered, (Tough, forthcoming a).

But the majority of staff in nursery schools and classes are not teachers at all, they are nursery assistants, usually with NNEB qualifications. These staff play a very major role in determining the quality of the children's educational experience. Many may find it difficult to guide children in their activities in a way which is purposeful, systematic and also informal. They may find difficulty in keeping track of children's progress, in making the best use of learning opportunities which arise, and in making the best use of their time to provide help and guidance to all the children in a class. For these assistants and also many teachers, it may be that some more formal guidance would be valuable. By familiarizing themselves fully with a programme with specific objectives and defined stategies, staff might be helped to grasp the underlying principles of structuring children's activities, of providing a thematic, sequenced, balanced and progressing programme. By working with a small, more manageable group they might discover the benefits for the children of sustained involvement in various activities. Once the basic principles have been assimilated then the constraints of formality can be thrown off, leaving the staff in a better position to control and make use of the 'structure' intrinsic to the informal education environment.

Chapter VI

Intervention through the family

The nursery only plays a small part in any child's life. Undoubtedly the limited and short term success of nursery programmes, however well planned, is mainly due to the pervasive effect of a multitude of influences on children's development other than their school experience. The major socializing influence on the child comes from his family. It has been argued that for real success the nursery must not only work with the child, but also with his parents. Working with parents can serve to ensure continuity in children's experience of home and school. Parents can be helped to understand the work of the nursery, which may enable them to reinforce the skills acquired at school through the environment they provide at home. And discussions between parents and teachers enable the teacher better to recognize any unique difficulties which may face the children.

This general mutually informing function of parental involvement has always been recognized by nursery practitioners. Indeed the circumstances of the nursery are especially suited for providing a basis of co-operation between home and school. Parents usually escort their young child to the nursery, and collect him at the end of a session (or arrange for a relative, neighbour, or friend to do so). These daily visits provide excellent opportunities for informal discussions with the head and her staff. Additionally the small size and informal atmosphere of the nursery is more inviting to parents who might otherwise be hesitant about entering what to them may be the threatening or even awesome atmosphere of their child's school.

The Plowden Report reiterated the importance of this type of parental involvement in promoting co-operation between school and parents, but added to this a rather different function:

'Nursery education should throughout be an affair of co-operation between the nursery and home and it will only succeed to the full if it carries the parents into partnership. Support does not mean mild consent; it means the kind of active concern which can only come out of joint activity and out of close knowledge by the parents of what the schools are doing and why. The nursery group needs to be an outpost of adult education if it is to attain its goal for young children.'

(Central Advisory Council for Education, 1967, Vol. 1, para. 320.)

The proposal that the nursery should actively promote parent education stems from recognition that the school is only one influence on the child's psychological development. For the major part of his life the child is in the care of his parents and their attitude to and understanding of the educational process will have an important influence on his school success. Some have tried to quantify the relative importance of home and school. A study reported by the Plowden Committee (Central Advisory Council for Education, 1967, Vol. II Appendices 3 and 4) concluded that 'parental attitude' is more important than 'home circumstances' or 'state of school' in determining children's level of educational attainment. Such statements are based on complex statistical analyses (in this case regression analysis) and have a very specific and restricted meaning. Like so many statistical statements about the importance of a variable to attainment the result is liable to misinterpretation and misuse. We have already mentioned two other similar statements which are often misinterpreted: Bloom's 'the importance of the first five years' (Bloom, 1964); and Jensen's 'the importance of heredity and environment' (Jensen, 1969):

Perhaps more valuable than establishing precise numerical statements of the importance of environmental factors, in this case parental attitudes, is to understand the way in which these attitudes affect the child and his response to school experiences. A famous study by Hess and Shipman (1965) has described the way parent attitudes mediate the style of mother-child communication in a learning situation. The study was conducted with American Negro mothers but some of the insights about parent's intuitive skill as teachers are likely to be equally relevant to the British context.

The mothers were interviewed and then systematically observed interacting with their four-year-old children. Simple tasks were demonstrated to the mother who was then asked to teach them to her child. Clear differences in style of interaction emerged related to the social class of the parent. Children of working class homes were less skilled at the tasks, and their parents were less proficient in teaching them.

Two extracts quoted by Hess and Shipman from interaction in the context of a block-sorting task illustrate these differences.

'*Mother — Child A*

Mother 'A' "All right, Susan, this board is the place where we put the little toys; first of all you're supposed to learn how to place them according to color. Can you do that? The things that are all the same color you put in one section; in the second section you put another group of colors and in the third section you put the last group of colors. Can you do that? Or would you like to see me do it first?"

Child 'A' "I want to do it."'

'*Mother — Child B*

Mother 'B' "Now I'll take them all off the board; now you put them all back on the board. What are these?"

Child 'B' "A truck."

Mother 'B' "All right, just put them right here; put the other one right here; all right put the other one there."'

(Hess & Shipman, 1965)

The first mother used speech to label and identify objects and their qualities, and made the rationale of the task explicit. The second mother used speech merely to give specific directions for the child's action. These are examples of general differences which appear to be related to social class; the middle class mothers were more able to anticipate the course of the child's learning, organize the task accordingly into small steps, recognize their child's difficulties, take steps to guide his action, and praise his successes. In short the middle class mothers made much greater use of the potential of speech to plan and direct activity. Their style of interaction was much closer than the working class mothers to the teaching methods found in the nursery.

Clearly, this research has relevance to the aims and methods of compensatory education. Classroom programmes can only have a limited influence on the child's development and need to be supported by work with parents to modify the child's educational experiences at home. To be truly successful compensatory education would have to harness the influence of the parent to the goal of the school.

For some research projects work with parents has been designed to complement a classroom programme. Others have taken a more extreme position and interpreted the relatively greater importance of parents as indicating that the most fruitful type of intervention will be with parents *rather than* with the child.

One other consideration favours this latter view. The parent has a continuous influence on the socialization of her child, whereas the influence of a nursery programme is essentially short term. If the parent's attitude and understanding can be improved then this might potentially have a much longer-term effect. Two main strategies of parent education have been submitted to some evaluation and will be considered in turn. The first uses the school as a base and context for working with parents. The second works within the home to provide activities for children and discussion with parents.

School-based parent education

The proposal that nursery schools and classes should be centres for parent education, places quite a different perspective on the normal view of parental involvement. It has implications for the type of parent involved in the work of the nursery, and the nature of their involvement. Although no research data are available for nursery schools and classes, it is probable that the parents who have traditionally been the most eager and able to support the nursery and acceptable to the staff working in it, already possess considerable understanding of the importance of education, whilst the group of parents who might benefit most are less likely to come forward and more difficult to accommodate within the organization of the nursery. Clearly, Plowden's proposal places an onus on the school to promote the involvement of this second group of parents.

The type of involvement which parents are most happy to offer, and schools to accept, has traditionally been supportive of the main work in the classroom (fund-raising, helping on outings etc.). But if parental involvement is to be viewed as parent education, it requires the staff to make a more active effort, either to involve the parents directly in classroom activities or to discuss issues in child development with them. Time spent supervising parents, tends to be time when the children are neglected, or so nursery staff may perceive it.

These then appear to be some of the problems facing any scheme to use the school as a base for parent education. Briefly stated they add up to the question of how to design a scheme which is within the resources of the school and can be operated by the staff without detracting unduly from their normal work, and then how to encourage parents to participate in it.

Perhaps it is these practical dilemmas, never mind the problem of how to evaluate such a scheme, which seem so effectively to have discouraged researchers from taking on the task. In her book on the subject, Anne Sharrock (1970, p. 119) draws special attention to the dearth of research on the subject, and the situation appears to have altered little since then. A considerable amount of research has been conducted in the American context; we shall come to a little of this later. With respect to the British situation we must rely on the NFER 'Pre-School Project', one small part of which designed to explore strategies of parent education (Woodhead, 1976, Chap. II).

An experiment in parental involvement (NFER)

One of the nursery schools involved in the evaluation of the Peabody Language Development Kit (it provided some children for both experimental and control groups) was selected as the context for work with parents. This nursery serves the families who live on a council estate close to Slough's industrial estate. Prior to the project's involvement, contact with parents had been restricted to the daily delivery and collection of children and occasional social events and jumble sales.

The project team had no pre-conceived plan for a 'parent programme'; and there were few reports available of previous research, the successes and failures of which might have guided the formulation of a strategy. Consequently the work with parents represented successive attempts to explore various approaches to parent education, initial attempts leading to more refined and focussed plans.

Considerable difficulties would have resulted from trying to design a precise evaluation of these approaches. In view of their diffuse objectives and diverse methods, reliable conclusions about effects on parent's attitude and children's attainment would have been difficult to obtain. Instead the project relied on more subjective evidence of the opinions of nursery staff and attitudes of parents.

The first approach was through a series of meetings, held in the adjoining primary school because of the shortage of space in the nursery. An initial meeting to inform parents about the project was followed by a series of five monthly talks by members of the project team and discussions on themes relating to the development and education of the pre-school child. These were held during the morning and afternoon and were attended by a small proportion of the parents of children at the nursery, about 15 parents on average per meeting.

At the end of the series of meetings, the headmistress of the nursery reported that although parents seemed to have enjoyed the discussions, in practice they seemed to learn more from doing something than from talking about it. Consequently the second approach taken by the team was to encourage active involvement by parents in the nursery classroom, to observe the work of staff, discuss it with them and participate in children's activities. Two parents at a time were invited to spend one session per week for a month in one of the two nursery classes. Initial doubts and hesitancy expressed by some of the 10 mothers who participated were soon dispelled as they relaxed in the informal happy atmosphere of the nursery. Regular attendance by a small number of mothers was felt to increase the mutual understanding of parents and staff alike. In particular the parents were able to learn from staff the value of play-activities to their children's development.

The third approach to parent-education sought to reinforce this recognition of the value of activities. Weekly Creative Activity Sessions were held during which a small group of mothers was encouraged to make imaginative use of household materials. It was hoped that through their own efforts mothers would discover skills in themselves which they could then transmit to their children through similar play at home.

Finally, the nursery school developed a library scheme. The County Library provided a large number of books which were then loaned to children to take home and enjoy with their parents. The parents were encouraged to help choose the books, and read them to their children at home. This aspect of the project was a great success and has continued long after the completion of the research.

This account illustrates some of the variety of approaches which have been taken to parent education in the nursery school. They are in many ways complementary. In the first approach the emphasis is on learning through discussion, in the second through observing, and finally through doing.

Although no formal evaluation of this project was possible, such evaluations have been attempted in similar research conducted in the USA. For example Karnes (1968) described a project in which working class Negro mothers were initiated into methods of stimulating cognitive growth in their three- to four-year-old children. The short term effects of a 12 week programme were evaluated in terms of changes in the children's cognitive and language ability (measures by Stanford-Binet and Illinois Test of Psycholinguistic Abilities). Thirteen children and their mothers who underwent the programme were compared with a matched control group. The programme was quite similar to some aspects of that provided in the NFER Project. Mothers were taught to use household materials to make toys and games which they were asked to introduce to their children at home. Comparison of scores on pre- and post-testing indicated significantly greater improvement by the programme than by the comparison children.

Encouraging as these results are, it must be emphasized that the effects were short-term and no follow-up was made after termination of the training programme. Long-term success is likely to depend on the continued motivation of parents to devise new activities and spend time playing with their children. In this context it is significant to note that unlike the NFER project, which relied on mothers volunteering to participate for the benefit of themselves and their children, the mothers in Karnes' project were paid to attend the training sessions and were informed that their purpose was to develop and try out activities for pre-school children. Although participation in the project may have improved their appreciation of the design of children's activities, the heightened motivation to be interested in their children may have quickly dissipated once the financial incentive and external rationale to do so had been removed.

The Karnes study evaluated effects of a parent programme on the children. A project by Gray and Klaus (1965) provides an illustration of the potential effects on the mother. These mothers were invited to observe their children in a pre-school centre, were explained the educational relevance of activities and eventually encouraged to participate actively in the pre-school programme. After several months these mothers were found to have improved their scores on an adult intelligence test and were also observed to have developed an educational orientation to the use of situations outside the classroom.

These results indicate that working with parents may be a valuable alternative to classroom programmes. So far only programmes based outside the home have been described; an alternative approach is to work with mothers and children in their normal home environment.

Home-based Parent Education

Home visiting is not considered simply as an alternative approach to involving parents in the education of their children; it offers some unique advantages and has characteristics distinct from school-based parental involvement.

The most fundamental problem for any classroom-based parent programme is to encourage the parents to attend the school.

For many parents this would not be possible; their children attend the nursery because their mother is obliged to work or because there are pressing problems of caring for other young children in what may be difficult home circumstances. Other parents may be reluctant to enter the classroom. Their own experiences at school may have made them wary of entering their child's school and encountering teacher. This wariness may be combined with uncertainty about what their role would be, a feeling that it is the teachers who are paid to care for their children, or quite simply a desire for a few hour's relief. Many of these parents might have something to learn from a parent programme, but are least likely to feel able or willing to attend.

There is also another group who make least use of pre-school services. These are the parents whose children do not attend any pre-school centre because of the ignorance, apathy, or inability of the parents. Home visiting provides a unique opportunity to make contact with these groups, and work within the context of their home to encourage their interest in and knowledge of their children's development and how best it may be fostered.

Home visiting also overcomes some of the difficulties experienced by teachers in their efforts to reconcile the conflict between the demands made on them by children and by parents in the classroom. They may feel that time spent with parents is time lost from children. By visiting the parent and child at home the educational visitor can concentrate all her efforts on providing guidance appropriate to their individual circumstances. Additionally, children do not normally attend nursery provision until they are three or four. Home visiting offers the opportunity to intervene in the educational experiences of the very young children, by influencing the parents' attitudes from the start.

An experiment in home-visiting (West Riding EPA)

There is ample evidence that parents are interested in their children's education. What they often lack is an understanding of the process and a recognition of their own role in it. The West Riding EPA scheme attempted to enhance mothers' understanding of their contribution to their children's development (Smith, 1975, Chap. 9). The project concentrated on mothers with children under three years old. A three month pilot study which indicated that mothers' reaction to being visited was favourable was followed by a two year scheme in which 20 mothers and children were visited and any changes in the children's ability and home environment evaluated by comparison with a similar control group.

The project team were acutely aware of the potential danger of the visitor antagonizing a mother. The visitor might be perceived as threatening, as criticizing the mother's child-rearing practices. Consequently the emphasis throughout the scheme was on working with mothers towards a mutual understanding of the particular child's development.

The scheme was initially introduced to parents as investigating young children's experiences at home and what they had learned before entering school. Accordingly early visits were spent asking the mother about the child, his development, and the mother's expectations for him. It very soon became apparent that the mothers tended not to recognize that they were instrumental in determining the child's acquisition of motor, cognitive and language skills. Rather, these skills were expected to mature in the natural course of time. For many of these mothers 'learning' was the province of the school, and they were reluctant to do anything which might interfere with the child's later school experiences. The mothers' sense of impotence about what they regarded as 'school learning' may account for their limited expectations for their children's development at home. As a result of their discussions, the West Riding team concluded that the mothers eagerly encouraged the children to develop physical agility but placed much less emphasis on the fine motor skills, such as using a pencil and paintbrush, or playing with jigsaws and similar puzzles. Further, the mothers tended not to recognize the value of books, and considered them inappropriate for children of this age.

The intervention strategy was adapted to the particular circumstances of a family and the attitude of the mother. In general, the visitors worked closely with the mother and demonstrated what her child was capable of and how he could best be helped. A small number of toys and games were introduced at each of the weekly visits. The children were encouraged to complete each activity before commencing the next and special attention was paid to developing the relationship between mother and child, to encourage independent play from the child who was over-dependent on the mother for directions, and, at the other extreme, to encourage greater co-operation from the child who was resentful of the mother's interference if she tried to involve herself in his play. Thus the visits were designed to provide a programme of activities to develop fine motor, cognitive and language abilities in the child, and at the same time to equip the mother with skills which would enable her to reinforce and follow-up the programme throughout the week, and also increase her long term understanding of how best she could help her child through his primary schooling.

The home visting scheme was evaluated for 20 boys and girls, who were compared with a control group of children of similar home background. The average age of the children when the scheme began was nearly two years old. Accurate psychometric assessments of such young children are notoriously difficult to make and are considerably less reliable than when the children are older. The West Riding team chose to use the Merrill-Palmer Scale which is designed to test general ability, as well as making more informal assessments of development. Both types of assessment pointed to the value of the scheme for the children. There were no significant differences on pre-testing, but by the end of the first year of the scheme the children who had been visited at home showed a significant advantage which was largely maintained through the second year.

Unfortunately it is not possible to make a valid comparison between this result and that found for the evaluation of nursery-based programmes. The ages of the children were different and so were the criterion measures used. Certainly, both types of programme appear to have beneficial short-term effects for the children's development.

However it is perhaps more useful to evaluate the unique features of the home visiting scheme. Home-based schemes might be expected potentially to have greater long term benefits for the children than a nursery programme. The children move on from a special nursery programme, which may or may not be reinforced by subsequent school experiences. By contrast any influence of the home-visiting *on the parents* may be reflected in the home environment provided for the children throughout their school career.

The classroom programmes we have discussed in Chapter III were not found to have substantial long term effects. Unfortunately within the West Riding it was not possible to follow-up the children after the end of the home visting scheme. However, the project did try to assess its effects on the children's home environment. Rating scales were completed at the end of the first year for all the homes of experimental and control groups. The scales covered the quality of the educational environment (e.g. toys and books) and the relationship of mother and child (e.g. initiative shown by the child, interest shown by the mother). The results were not conclusive; generally they did not favour the home visiting scheme having greatly influenced the home environment of the children. The exceptions were an increase in visual material found in the homes of the experimental children and less use by mothers of negative sanctions in controlling children's behaviour.

These results support those described for school-based parent education programmes. There are short-term influences on the parents' behaviour and consequently the children's test performance, but longer term influences on the parents' educational attitude and behaviour towards their children are more difficult to establish. However there is one very comprehensive evaluation of a parent education programme which does show long term benefits. This was conducted as part of the Early Education Program, Ypsilanti, Michigan, and is reported by Radin (1972). The study compared different types and amounts of parental participation in children's education. Three groups of approximately 20 children were selected from the four-year-olds attending the pre-school programme. Four different educational strategies were used. The mothers of Group 'A' were most intensively involved. Besides the normal programme (Strategy I) the children were visited at home twice a week by a teacher who introduced activities to the children (II) and encouraged the mother to participate and reinforce them during the rest of the week (III). Additionally mothers of these children were invited to attend weekly small group discussions on child-development (IV). In the other groups, mothers were less involved. For Group 'B' strategies included I, II and III but not IV; for Group 'C' strategies included I and II but not III or IV.

A comprehensive battery of instruments was used to assess the effects of the scheme. After one year children in all the groups had made significant gains on a test of general ability (Stanford-Binet) and vocabulary (Peabody Picture Vocabulary test). However no differences were found between the groups which might have suggested different effects of degrees of maternal involvement. Similarly, no differences were apparent in the children's classroom behaviour as rated by the teacher.

However, questionnaires administered to the parents to assess the home environment provided for their children and their attitude to their education did produce a few differences. Group 'A' showed a significant increase in the provision of educational materials and a decrease in authoritarian attitude to their children. This is a similar result to the increase in visual materials and decrease in negative sanctions described for the West Riding Study (page 89). Group 'B' only showed an increase in educational expectation for their children, while no changes had occurred for Group 'C', who had been least involved.

Follow-up of the children one year after the programme showed that differential effects of parent involvement may have affected the parents' relation to the child in the long term. Although no difference was apparent at the end of the programme, a year later there were differences between the groups on the vocabulary test, which were statistically significant between 'B' and 'C'. No differences were found on a test of general ability. Perhaps not surprisingly, the more parents are involved in their children's pre-school education the greater will be its likely benefits.

The West Riding Home Visiting Scheme is one of many which have proliferated in recent years (outlined by Tizard, B., 1975). It was described at some length as an illustration of the approach because it has the virtue of having been subjected to quite rigorous evaluation. Many of the schemes which are currently being set up by local authorities have a much smaller built-in research element. Co-ordinated evaluation of these schemes is urgently needed before the effectiveness of the strategy can be properly assessed. From the small number of studies described here it seems probable that the advocates of parent programmes may have overestimated the long-term changes in parent behaviour which a short term project can produce, just as the advocates of special nursery programmes had overestimated their potential influence on the child. In both cases the interventionists have failed to recognize the multitude of other influences on the mother and child, which are far more pervasive than a few hours of a special programme.

All too often what is not recognized is that successful intervention depends not only on teaching the child and mother skills they did not previously possess, but changing the deep-seated attitudes of which their cognitive and linguistic styles are merely superficial mani- festations. The home experiences of children, their life-style and expectations, are a product of and adapted to their social circum- stances. Consequently, an educational programme for mother or child is only likely to have real success if it is long-term and sustained throughout the child's school experience.

In practice it is probable that home visiting is not a rival approach to pre-school education, but complements it. Disadvantaged families who are unable or reluctant to ensure that their children attend pre-school provision are particularly likely to benefit from an educational home visitor, as are those where the very youngest children appear to be at risk.

It is important to recognize the dangers of adding yet another visitor to the list of representatives of welfare and educational agencies who might call on these disadvantaged families. Although the professionals may recognize the subtle differences in role and function between the social worker, health visitor and educational home visitor, the families are less likely to make the necessary differentiation and may resent repeated intrusions from different 'visitors', none of whom may appear capable or willing to provide a solution to their particular current problem, preoccupied as the visitors tend to be with their own particular 'chunk' of the welfare and education domain. The resentment may be exacerbated by the lack of co-ordination which may result from the visitors being based in different agencies, social services, general practitioners and education departments respectively. An alternative approach which co-ordinates the efforts of all these agencies and the school might prove much more effective. One alternative which is gaining in popularity is 'community education'.

An alternative model — community education

The parent schemes which have been described adhere quite closely to a compensatory model which recognizes a role for the school in making up for deficiencies in the child's home experiences. However, strong arguments have been expressed against this 'unilateral' approach to the education of the disadvantaged child and his parents, as denying the relevance of these children's experiences and seeking to make them middle class (Poulton and James, 1975, p. 27). This approach argues that the child's failure and the parents' alienation from school is not simply a manifestation of the inability of the pupil and the inadequacy of the home, but also arises out of the discrepancy in values, expectations and experiences between home and school. The home environment of the working class child appears deficient only when it is assessed in terms of the predominantly middle class standards of the school.

The approach argues that the home experiences of these children can provide a firm basis for learning, and should not be undermined by the school trying to compensate for them. Instead they should be used as the foundation for providing an education which is relevant to the children. In this way the emphasis is shifted away from the inadequacies of the home towards the failures of the school. It is the school that must change to make the organization and curriculum more approriate to the community.

A great deal of the work of the EPA teams was directed towards promoting community education. One facet of this was to develop a curriculum based on experiences which would be familiar to the children. Chapter III has already described 'Dr. Wotever', a pre-school programme based on the adventures of two small boys in a block of flats in Liverpool (page 34). The other facet of 'community education' has been to explore methods of increasing the co-operation between parents and teachers, and extending their mutual understanding.

It would be artificial to try to split-off examples of this approach which are directly concerned with pre-school children; indeed to try to do so might be considered against the spirit of community education which, with its focus on serving the family as a unit, seeks to break down artificial barriers between stages in the continuous educational process. Much of the work which was particularly directed towards primary age children has equal relevance to the pre-school debate.

Broadly speaking, strategies of community education may be divided between those using the school as the centre for activity, (notably home-school liaison teachers) and those using a community centre, (in this case, West Riding EPA's 'Red House').

Experiments in home-school liaison (Birmingham, Deptford and Dundee EPA)

Experiments in home-school liaison were tried out in Birmingham, Deptford and Dundee. Two distinct roles seemed to develop for these visitors, that of the Home-School Liaison Teacher, and of the Educational Social Worker. The work of the Dundee Educational Social Worker is particularly relevant to the discussion. She was specifically concerned with pre-school children, her task being to establish liaison between the various forms of pre-school provision in the area and the families who might use that provision. Visiting the homes in the neighbourhood she was able to identify children who would especially benefit from pre-school provision, and advise parents on the availability and function of playgroups, nursery schools, etc. At the same time she was able to provide information and advice to the playgroups on how best to provide for these children. In the current state of partial and largely unco-ordinated provision such local liaison is urgently needed, as we shall see in the final chapter. (More details of the Dundee scheme may be found in Educational Priority, Vol. V, Chap. 8 (Morrison *et al.*, 1974).

The home-school liaison teachers appointed in Birmingham and Deptford were based in the primary schools; indeed in the case of Deptford they were members of the school staff released from some teaching duties. Their general role was defined as increasing understanding between the school and the families served by it. The specific functions of the home-school liaison teachers varied but included visiting parents to sort out specific problems, collecting information about families, establishing the reasons for parents' visits to the school, and organizing exhibitions and activities for parents. The schemes were only evaluated subjectively but in some cases were quite successful. (They are described more fully in *Educational Priority* vol. 1., Chap. 9, Halsey, 1972.) The particular relevance of these schemes are the different roles they illustrate compared with that of the educational home-visitor who is much more concerned with parent-education. Clearly no nursery school could afford to create these posts, but their functions might be carried out by an interested teacher or assistant, and in many cases are already being carried out at a purely informal level.

The Community Education Centre (West Riding EPA)

A different approach to increasing home-school links is exemplified by the West Riding Community Education Centre, Red House. Much of the EPA project's pre-school work was centred in Red House and since this centre served multiple functions, maximum contact between different parts of the community was ensured. Amongst these functions were short-term residential schemes for families with special problems, holiday programmes for children, a youth club for older children and intensive courses for junior school children using students from a local college of education.

The advantage of a community centre approach is that the same institution may serve a number of aspects of family education and welfare. The division of education into stages is avoided, and artificial barriers removed which hinder recognition of the fact that a child's behaviour at school is closely linked to problems faced by other members of his family which should perhaps be treated together. Further details of this experiment may be found in Chapters 12 and 13 of the West Riding EPA report. (Smith, 1975).

Conclusion

It is in the nature of research to separate off educational approaches according to their rationale and the model of education in society to which they are working. Thus we have contrasted 'compensatory education' with 'community education', and 'school-based parent education schemes' with 'home visiting schemes', and each has been evaluated on its own terms, in its own right. But in practice nursery staff cannot afford the luxury of such precise theories or controlled programmes. The teacher may simultaneously be adapting several of these methods to achieve a variety of aims. She will be seeking co-operation with parents, to learn from them and develop a nursery programme adapted to the community in which she is working. But she will also strive to educate the parents to a better understanding of the goals of the school and how they can best further their children's progress. The teacher may invite parents into the school to observe the work of the nursery and discuss educational issues with her. Or she may in some cases feel it necessary to visit a mother and child at home, aware that one-to-one contact in the home environment offers special educational opportunities. What is most important is for the teachers at all times to recognize that the nursery programme is not the only nor necessarily the most important educational experience for the child. Only by being aware of these other influences and adapting the programme accordingly can the teacher claim to be concerned with the education of the 'whole child'.

One final point: in all that has been said so far 'parent' has been used almost as a synonym for 'mother'. All the studies have concentrated on working with the mothers of pre-school children. Although for many families the person spending most time with the child may be the mother, the contribution of the father to the child's socialization must not be underestimated. Initially the NFER scheme hoped to attract fathers to the nursery but this was not successful even though many of the local fathers were on shift work and could have come had they wished.

There are special reasons for seeking increased paternal involvement in the life of the nursery beyond that of parent-education. Many of the children are from single-parent families and lack a father-figure at home; at the same time nursery schools and classes tend to be woman-dominated establishments . Future attempts to evaluate parental involvement might do well to place special emphasis on increasing the presence of fathers or other male figures in the nursery.

Chapter VII

The first priority: Nursery provision for disadvantaged children

Readers of the previous chapters may be forgiven for feeling irritated by extended discussions of research designed to discover the *type of nursery programme* which is most likely to prove beneficial to disadvantaged children and their parents. At a time when the majority of such children experience *no nursery programme* at all, this kind of discussion may be construed as something of a luxury if not a complete irrelevancy. The first prerequisite for using pre-school education to enrich the learning experiences of disadvantaged children is to ensure that nursery places are made freely available to and taken-up by these children. The purpose of this chapter is to review research and recent developments in the provision of services for pre-school children, describe the current extent of services and suggest some ways in which they may be failing and might be improved.

Recent developments in pre-school provision

For an account of the early growth of pre-school provision the reader is referred to Blackstone (1971). Recent developments may most conveniently be traced to the recommendations of the Plowden Committee (Central Advisory Council for Education, 1967). The Plowden Committee's recommendations for expansion were two-pronged: nursery education was to be made more generally available, but resources for expansion were to be concentrated particularly in underprivileged areas.

A.H. Halsey has described the government's responses to these recommendations (Halsey, 1972, Chapter 3). The EPA concept was taken up by the Department of Education and Science which allocated extra resources for building and made an allowance for teachers working in the Priority areas. But, during the period until 1972, the major implementation of Plowden's proposals for EPAs resulted from joint action taken by three departments of government (The Home Office, Ministry of Health and Department of Education and Science). This was the Urban-Aid scheme which provided for expenditure over four years of up to £25,000,000 on housing, health, education and welfare facilities in deprived areas. The scheme has subsequently been extended through several phases, and a major part of the resources has been allocated to nursery education; Halsey reports that by the end of 1971, 18,000 new nursery places had ben approved under the Urban Programme.

In 1972 this limited expansion in Priority Areas was overtaken by the government's plans for the general provision of nursery education facilities. These were contained in the White Paper *Education: A Framework for Expansion* (DES, 1972) and subsequently in *Circular 2/73* (DES, 1973). In large measure these proposals reflected the detailed recommendations of the Plowden committee. The Government recommended to local education authorities (LEAs) that expansion should take the form of nursery classes attached to primary schools. 1982 was set as the target for achieving Plowden's goal of nursery education for all children whose parents want it. In practice, it was estimated that 250,000 new full-time equivalent places would be required to satisfy an assumed demand from 50 per cent of three-year-olds and 90 per cent of four-year-olds. Most children would be able to attend part-time (either mornings or afternoons) only, although sufficient full-time places would be made available to accommodate 15 per cent of each year group. Clearly these proposals extend beyond the limited aim of using nursery education as positive discrimination to help disadvantaged children. This is a proposal for nursery education for all who want it. The Government did however recognize a continuing compensatory role for nursery education:

> 'Nursery education is particularly valuable as a means of reducing the educational and social disadvantages suffered by children from homes which are culturally and economically deprived.'
>
> (DES, 1973, para. 9)

To monitor the development of the new provision the DES proposed to set up a Nursery Education Research Programme (NERP) the progress of which has been described by Kay (1975).

As a reference against which to examine developments in pre-school services, it may be useful to describe the provision which was available at the time when implementation of the government's proposals began. Nursery education (in the form of nursery schools and classes) was only available to nine per cent of three- and four-year-olds, plus a very small percentage of two-year-olds, in England and Wales in January,

Table 2: **Maintained educational provision for the under-fives — January, 1974 (England and Wales)**

	Nursery schools	*Nursery classes*	*Primary school classes*
Number	584	2,410	—
Children:			
Full-time	15,431	32, 527	268,693
Part-time	30,401	61,762	16,210
Total	45,832	94,289	284,903

(DES, 1974, Table 27)

Figure 5: **Three- and four-year-olds attending maintained educational provision — January, 1974 (England and Wales)**

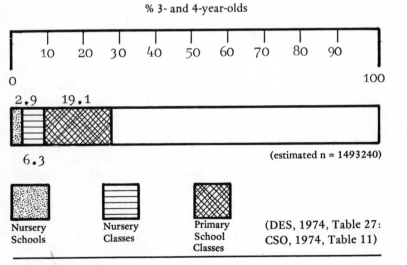

% 3- and 4-year-olds

(estimated n = 1493240)

Nursery Schools   Nursery Classes   Primary School Classes

(DES, 1974, Table 27: CSO, 1974, Table 11)

1974 (Table 2; Fig. 5). The remaining 19 per cent in school are all early
admissions to the reception classes of primary schools (which have a
lower ratio of staff to children than true nursery establishments).
Accordingly this group is made up almost exclusively of four-year-olds,
and 60 per cent are rising five.

Although the government's proposals for expansion of nursery
education do not have any direct implications for social services or
voluntary provision, any major expansion programme would of course
have a substantial effect on the demand for these other services. Day
nurseries, which offer all-day care for 'special cases' are the only type of
maintained provision, but additionally social services departments have
responsibility for supervising the very large numbers of private
nurseries, playgroups and child-minders (Table 3).

Table 3: Social Services provision for the under-fives — March, 1973 (England)

| | Maintained | Voluntary | |
	Day nurseries	Registered nurseries	Registered child minders
Number	488	12,834	30,020
Places	23,718	322,347	90,227

(DHSS, 1974a)

These national figures present only a very limited picture of the
services available for the under-fives. They tend to blur the very big
differences in provision across the country. Local demand has varied in
different areas, and education authorities have differed in their
sensitivity to it. Thus figures reported in *Education*, 18th January,
1974 show that in January, 1973 (under old local authorities
boundaries) Carnaevonshire and Leicester City were top of the league
with about 42 per cent of three- and four-year-olds in nursery schools
and classes; the list of authorities with less than two per cent is too long
to mention. These figures are only of nursery schools and classes; it
must be remembered that some authorities have adopted a policy of
admitting chldren full-time to reception classes of primary schools at
four; and in some areas, the playgroup movement is stronger than
others.

Not only does the amount of provision differ between local
authorities, the balance of various forms of provision is specific to each

Figure 6: Attendance at pre-school provision in an inner-city and a rural area

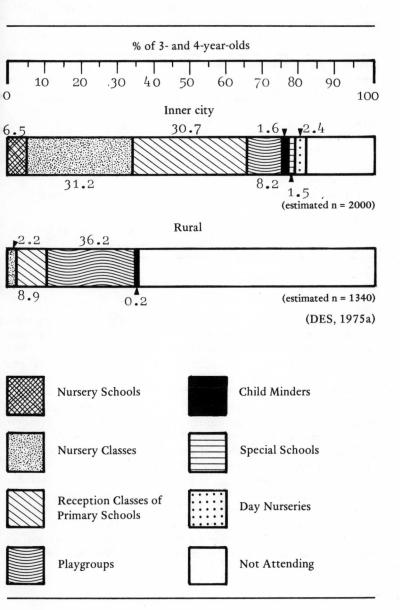

% of 3- and 4-year-olds

Inner city

(estimated n = 2000)

Rural

(estimated n = 1340)

(DES, 1975a)

Nursery Schools

Child Minders

Nursery Classes

Special Schools

Reception Classes of Primary Schools

Day Nurseries

Playgroups

Not Attending

local authority area. The short-term studies conducted during 1974 as part of the DES Nursery Education Research Programme made a comparison between small districts within six local authorities. The pattern of provision in two is presented as Figure 6.

Although it is too early to assess the impact of the Government's expansion programme on the extent of nursery provision, some increases are already discernible from the most recent figures, Table 4.

Table 4: Nursery education in England

	January 1974	*January, 1975*	*Increase*
Places			
full-time			
equivalent	80,369	88,701	8,332
Children			
attending			
full-time	37,148	38,575	1,427
attending			
part-time	86,443	100,253	13,810

(Figures reported in *Education* 21.11 1975)

But the prospects for the expansion programme in the coming years are bleak. On current population trends, the total number of full-time equivalent places required to achieve the Government's target for 1982 is estimated as 510,000 (*Education*, 21.11.75). A series of setbacks in the programme makes it extremely unlikely that this target will even be approached by 1982.

The first setback has been the reduction by the Government of the allocation for capital expenditure from approximately £40 million over the two years 1974—76, to merely £9 million for 1976—7. Another problem has been the failure of some local authorities to make the capital expenditure on nursery building projects which has been sanctioned by the government. At a time when the costs of maintaining already existing educational provision have increased enormously, and have not adequately been offset by increased revenue, local authorities have been reluctant to take on new ventures which would inevitably commit them to further recurrent expenditure. Indeed local authorities have been encouraged by the Government to make economies wherever possible, Circular 10/75 (DES, 1975c). Consequently, in response to a parliamentary question (reported in *Education*, 7.11.75) the Secretary of State, Mr Fred Mulley, announced that 22 local education authorities had relinquished either all or part of their nursery education building allocation for 1975—76. One local authority has even threatened to close down existing nursery provision (reported in *Times Educational Supplement* 31.10.75). The effect of some LEAs failing to expand nursery education provision can only be to make the pattern of provision across the country even more varied than it has hitherto been. Some ways in which 13 local authorities have developed provision under current economic constraints is described in *Education*, 22.11.75.

Finally the latest Circular 10/75 (DES, 1975c) has recommended local authorities to reconsider their policies with regard to admission of children under five to primary schools except where nursery conditions are provided — conditions which demand, for example, a higher ratio of staff to children. This practice has increased in recent years such that there are now twice the number of under-fives in the reception classes of infant schools as in true nursery classes or schools (Table 2). If local authorities heed the Government's advice, and it is plain that some are already doing so (*Times Educational Supplement*, 31.10.75), this would effectively reduce the number of school places for under-fives by two-thirds with major repercussions on the remaining 'true' nursery establishments. These would most likely feel obliged to cater primarily for the older children in the under-five group (i.e. four-year-olds). It may be predicted that these measures would in turn dramatically increase the demand for voluntary provision, notably playgroups.

It is impossible to forecast the long term future for the expansion of pre—school provision. From observing current social trends it is plain that the demand will continue to increase. But it is equally plain that in the present economic climate, expenditure on improving the supply of places will be increasing at a considerably slower rate.

Under these circumstances it is all the more imperative that what revenues are available be spent wisely. For local authorities this means as far as possible making the best use of existing facilities, by adapting primary school buildings, rather than building expensive new units. Local authorities are well used to making these economies. Additionally they might look to further ways of supporting existing voluntary provision. But most important of all, measures are urgently needed which will ensure that the few new nursery places made available are in the correct location and of the most appropriate type to suit the circumstances of families for whose children the new provision is intended. All too often social and educational planning is based at best on a series of educated guesses. As an illustration of this we may observe the reasoning behind Plowden's influential recommendations about the extent and type of nursery education which would be needed, based on a series of 'assumptions' many of which are now open to doubt (Central Advisory Council for Education, 1967, Vol. 1, para. 328).

Here is a very important role for research. Research is required to monitor the changing needs of young children and their families in relation to the pre-school services made available, any discrepancies which become apparent forming the basis for further general planning as well as specific innovations. This type of research is required at a local as well as a national level; national prescriptions for pre-school services are likely to have limited local applicability. Numerous small-scale studies have been completed by local authorities, Pre-school Playgroups Association and other bodies concerned with provision for the under-fives. Most have been designed to guide the development of provision at a local level and therefore findings have not been published or widely distributed. Two examples of local studies which have been reported are (Honey, Neale *et al.*, 1973) and Lozells Social Development Centre (1975).

Amongst major studies which are currently underway or nearing completion is, for example, one in Birmingham being conducted by members of the Department of Social and Administrative Studies, University of Oxford. Members of The Department of Child Health, University of Bristol, are conducting a massive national study, the 'Child Health and Education in the Seventies Project'. A model for this type of research is provided by a project in New Zealand conducted by David Barney (1975).

Unfortunately it will be some time before the results of this research are available. In the meantime, the remainder of this chapter will draw on the research and statistics which are available and can be used to highlight the state of existing pre-school provision and pinpoint any apparent anomalies. As before the general theme of the discussion will be the suitability of provision for children from disadvantaged home backgrounds.

Educational provision for disadvantaged children

Although we have general statistics for the various types of pre-school provision there is a dearth of information about the children served by them and the reasons they are attending one kind rather than another. Our interest here is particularly in whether the most disadvantaged children are gaining access to some form of nursery education experience. To obtain this information would require a detailed nationwide survey of the social background and circumstances of nursery children. Some of the studies already mentioned should eventually provide information of this kind. But for the present we must rely on more general surveys.

As a very crude indicator we may draw on the results of a national survey conducted by the Office of Population, Censuses and Surveys in 1971 (OPCS, 1973). The survey collected information about the occupation of the head of household, and the attendance of any of the under-fives at some form of pre-school provision. The results are presented as Figure 7. There is a clear trend which favours more of the children from higher social groups gaining admission to some form of provision than those from lower social groups. And the pattern is repeated within the two types of provision — nursery schools and classes; and day nurseries and playgroups. Since we know that within the lower social groups there is likely to be a higher proportion of socially disadvantaged children this distribution of nursery places can only serve to increase these children's disadvantage and perpetuate the inequalities between social groups.

It is unfortunate that the figures do not make a finer distinction between types of nursery. Broadly speaking the distinction between the two categories conforms to their administration by the education and social services departments of central and local government. It is probable that the figure for nursery schools and classes includes all children attending school before the age of five and does not separate nursery classes with nursery staffing ratios etc. from reception classes with infant school staffing ratios. The inclusion of independent schools also distorts the picture a little. We would expect these to cater for children from middle class backgrounds. However their numbers are small, approximately 100 compared with 3,000 maintained establishments (DES, 1974) which is not sufficient to account for the trend favouring the more advantaged groups. This finding needs substantiating by more detailed research. However it certainly suggests that on a national basis, the policy of paying special attention to providing nursery places for disadvantaged children may not be realized in practice, or was not in 1971.

If it had been possible to use more refined categories a different trend might have been expected for playgroups compared with day nurseries. In most cases playgroups cater particularly for children from higher social groups, with the exception of a few set up especially to cater for disadvantaged children (often sponsored by charitable organizations, e.g. NSPCC or Save the Children Fund). By contrast the function of day nurseries is to cater for children who need day long care by virtue of the circumstances of their homes, or the necessity of their mother taking up employment. When a composite is created from the two categories the dominant trend reflects the much higher incidence of playgroups than day nurseries.

Despite these limitations in the design of the study, these results do

Figure 7: Attendance at pre-school provision by socioeconomic group*

*Data for 1971, National Sample of over 15,000 households.

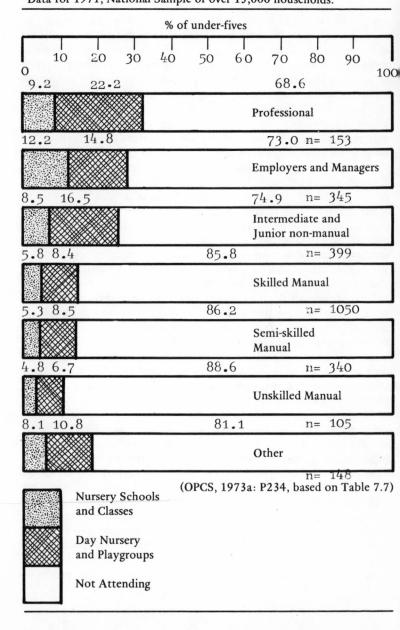

(OPCS, 1973a: P234, based on Table 7.7)

suggest that overall a much higher proportion of children from more 'advantaged' social groups are benefiting from some kind of pre-school experience; and specifically that LEA maintained provision may be failing to achieve the objective of enriching the early learning experiences of children from disadvantaged home circumstances.

These are national figures. Although we may suspect that the tendency for disadvantaged children to be less well catered for will have some generality, the specific pattern of take-up of places is likely to reflect the character of an area and the amount, type and distribution of pre-school provision which may be found in it.

The importance of examining the situation on a local as well as a national level is illustrated by the results of an early phase of the Bristol 'Child Health and Education in the Seventies' project. The investigation forms part of a longitudinal study of children born during one week in 1970. One region, South-West England and part of South Wales, was selected for study. Mothers of 1,000 children were interviewed and asked about their child's attendance at nursery. Figure 8 presents the results after they have been analysed in terms of an index of disadvantage/privilege, based on social class, parent education, housing conditions, family circumstances etc. (Osborn, 1975)

The general pattern of results is the same as for the national study. Overall the proportion of 'privileged' children who experience some kind of pre-school service is twice that of the 'disadvantaged' children. As we would expect this is largely due to the extensive use by the 'privileged' group of voluntary provision (playgroups and private nurseries). Maintained provision (schools and classes) is available to more disadvantaged than privileged children although the actual numbers involved are very small. In terms of ensuring that places are made available to the more disadvantaged children this is of course an encouraging trend, although it does conflict with the national picture of more 'privileged' children attending nursery schools and classes. We may suspect this is due to the particular circumstances of the region studied, a predominantly rural area where the few nursery schools and classes which have been opened are concentrated in the poorer districts of towns. Additionally the result may be age-specific. The information was collected when the children were three-and-a-half years. Many children are not admitted to nurseries until they are four; the early admissions may include a larger number of 'priority cases'.

A great many more studies of this kind are required before we can make a proper evaluation of the adequacy of pre-school provision at a local and national level. But clearly, despite the availability of new nursery places under the Urban Aid programme, the overall imbalance of take-up of nursery places has not been redressed. It seems that for the present the desire to use nursery education for positive dis-

Figure 8: Family background of children and attendance at pre-school provision: a regional study

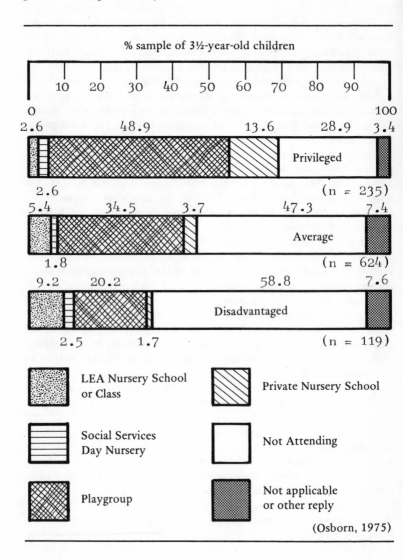

% sample of 3½-year-old children

(Osborn, 1975)

crimination must remain unfulfilled; it cannot be a practical possibility until steps are taken to ensure that the children most in need obtain places. Let us consider in a little more detail the reasons why this situation prevails and the lessons which may be learned from it for the future.

The concept of the Educational Priority Area (EPA)

One possibility is that local authorities have based their allocation of resources for nursery education on inadequate or misleading information. Appropriate allocation depends on identifying the children most in need, and making places available accordingly. Local authorities have made extensive use of the EPA concept, which provided the rationale and procedure for administration of Urban Aid funds and is still widely used today. The EPA concept is not without its critics and has particularly come under fire from one of the research teams working within the EPAs. An extensive and complex evaluation was conducted as part of the Deptford EPA research. The research team were part of the Inner London Educational Authority (ILEA) Research and Statistics Group and were able to make use of the large quantity of survey data collected on primary schools and children within the authority. One of the questions to which the team addressed themselves is crucial to the present discussion: What is the effectiveness of identifying educational priority *areas* and *schools* as a technique of reaching *individual* disadvantaged children?

Following the recommendations of the Plowden report the ILEA research group had developed an Index of Disadvantage which could be used to identify educational priority schools. The Plowden report identified the following factors as associated with their concept of 'cumulative deprivation' (Central Advisory Council for Education, 1967, Vol. I).

(a) Occupation (proportions in social groups IV and V, semi- and unskilled manual)
(b) Family size
(c) Supplements from the State
(d) Overcrowding and shared housing
(e) Poor school attendance and truancy
(f) Incidence of retarded, disturbed or handicapped pupils
(g) Incomplete families
(h) Children unable to speak English

The development of the Index required selecting convenient measures of these criteria based on information from a school or its catchment area (taken from Census small-area data). The measures were transformed into a uniform scale to permit computation of a summed score of school disadvantage. Using this procedure a rank order had been obtained of schools within the Authority. At the same time the research team developed a procedure to apply the same Plowden criteria to the identification of individual disadvantaged children in the same primary schools, using data from a questionnaire completed by their teacher. The details of these techniques are described in full in Part 7 of *Education Priority* Vol. 3 (Barnes, 1975).

The team proceeded to compare the two methods of identifying disadvantage, to evaluate the success of the school based index recommended by Plowden as a method of identifying individual children in special need. They found that in any one school identified as disadvantaged there was usually only a minority of disadvantaged children; when the results were collated only 16.8 per cent of the children in priority schools were disadvantaged. Looking at the results from another angle, of all the disadvantaged children within the total number of schools studied, only 28.2 per cent were in priority schools. Apparently, within Inner London at least, even if extra resources were allocated to all priority schools and areas, less than a third of disadvantaged children would experience the potential benefits. This occurs because the EPA Index depends on a statistical average of disadvantage within an area. Accordingly, its usefulness is restricted to identifying the most disadvantaged areas but it is not sensitive to the overall distribution of disadvantage across areas.

The implication, as far as the Deptford research team were concerned was that the Plowden method of applying positive discrimination is both crude and may be wasteful of resources:

'We believe that the results of this part of our analysis confront the policy of discrimination in favour of EPA schools with a paradox. It seems likely that the majority of disadvantaged children are not in disadvantaged areas, and the majority of children in disadvantaged areas are not disadvantaged. At the least this means that policies to assist disadvantaged schools or areas should not be seen as alternatives to policies which are focused on groups of children, whether these groups are to be identified in terms of single or combined indicators of need.'

(Barnes, 1975, p. 248).

A similar argument has been presented by Acland (1971).

Clearly these arguments are equally applicable to the allocation of resources for pre-school provision. A policy which takes a school or its catchment area as the basis for deciding its priority for pre-school provision will tend only to provide funds where there is the highest concentration of disadvantaged children and neglect other areas which, taken together, contain a larger number of disadvantaged children, but are more geographically dispersed.

However in defence of the Plowden Report's concept of the Educational Priority Area it should be borne in mind that its origins lay in the Committee's observation of a tendency for the poorest schools to be concentrated in the most disadvantaged areas:

> 'Thus the vicious circle may turn from generation to generation and the schools play a central part in the process, both causing and suffering cumulative deprivation.' (Central Advisory Council for Education, 1967, Vol 1, para. 32).

The Plowden recommendations were designed to improve the quality of schools, as one way in which positive discrimination might be applied. The question of whether these schools are attended exclusively by disadvantaged children is in many ways immaterial; poor schools may contribute to 'disadvantage' and are undesirable whoever attends them. Additionally the fact that the majority of disadvantaged children do not attend priority schools does not reduce the value of identifying priority schools. These children are widely distributed across other generally more advantaged areas where, as the Plowden report observed, the quality of schools tends to be higher, and consequently the attainment of disadvantaged children also tends to be slightly higher; a fact which is in fact supported by another part of the Deptford EPA analysis (Barnes, 1975, pp. 261–2).

The implication for allocation of pre-school resources is that concentration on priority areas may miss large numbers of priority children. But in practice these children may not be at such a great disadvantage. Perhaps the important characteristic of priority areas, which the arguments of the London EPA team do not recognize is that a high concentration of disadvantage is associated with, and may produce special problems which serve to increase, any individual family's disadvantage, i.e. they may suffer 'cumulative disadvantage'. Educational Priority Areas are often also areas with decaying housing where communities may be disrupted or destroyed as a consequence of urban redevelopment and renewal, where families are being rehoused in flats which provide little play space for their children, and where the consequent incidence of family disturbance may stretch the resources of a Social Services Department to the limit. It is surely better to be 'disadvantaged' in a suburb than in an inner city! In conclusion, although a policy of allocating pre-school resources by priority areas may not reach the majority of disadvantaged children, it will probably reach the most disadvantaged children.

The source of a good deal of the controversy lies in the failure of the Plowden Committee to separate out the different levels at which positive discrimination in education can operate. Clearly when a local education authority is faced with the problem of how to make the best use of scarce resources to build new schools, or improve the staffing and facilities in old ones, then a school or area-based policy is the only feasible one. This was the level at which the Plowden Committee was proposing positive discrimination. By contrast the arguments used by the Deptford EPA team make clear that their emphasis is on identifying groups of individual disadvantaged children. Accordingly their approach to positive discrimination would operate through the allocation of resources within schools and depend largely on the provision of special programmes such as those described in earlier chapters.

Once the focus of positive discrimination is on the individual or groups of children within the school, then the usefulness of indices of social disadvantage is indeed doubtful. The Deptford team found that although the average standard of reading was poorer in the priority schools, there were great variations within the schools and there was not a close relationship between low performance and the various criteria of disadvantage. A similar result is described for a smaller sample of schools by Ferguson *et al.* (1971) and used to argue that effective positive discrimination must rely on the teacher's ability to identify children with adverse home circumstances and the effects this may have in retarding their development.

Positive discrimination at this individual level must surely complement positive discrimination through provision of nursery places. Our concern in this chapter is with the latter issue: how can appropriate provision be made available to suit the circumstances of pre-school children and their families.

Despite the general usefulness of the EPA concept it does have a number of drawbacks. In particular it may lead to the blanket identification of all areas which match up to EPA criteria as facing the same problems, and correspondingly lead to a belief that there is some universal nursery prescription for children's disadvantage.

In practice EPAs vary quite considerably in their characteristics and the problems they face. One of the early tasks of the EPA research teams was to collect a mass of general data on the areas in which they were working. The sources for these data were the 1966 Census, a survey of primary schools and staff, and assessments of the vocabulary and reading performance of the children. Details of these studies may be found in *Educational Priority*, Vol. II (Payne, 1974) and Vol. I, Chapter V (Halsey, 1972). This summary will be restricted to the English EPA areas. All the areas shared common features including high proportions of semi- or unskilled workers, and small proportions of owner-occupiers compared with the national average. But there were also considerable differences, particularly between the inner city areas and the more stable working class community of the West Riding. For example there was a contrast in the population stability. Ninety-nine per cent of the West Riding population studied were indigenous compared with the inner city areas which had received a large influx of Irish and Commonwealth immigrants. Similarly, 16 per cent of Birmingham and 17 per cent of Deptford residents were newcomers to the area (within five years) compared with seven per cent in the West Riding. Overcrowding was a problem shared by the inner city areas, up to 35 per cent of households sharing a dwelling in Birmingham but very few in the West Riding.

In addition to differences between areas in the social circumstances of the families, differences were also found in the schools which their children attended. The staff in the EPA schools were generally found to be both young and inexperienced. Thirty-two per cent of Deptford teachers and 27 per cent of Birmingham teachers were under 25, compared with a figure for all maintained primary schools in England and Wales of 18 per cent. By contrast, only 10 per cent of West Riding staff were under 25, and 46 per cent were 45 years or over, rather older than the national average. Similarly the turnover of staff in the inner city areas was high; only a quarter of the staff had been at their schools for five years or more compared with half the West Riding staff

Clearly these differences in the nature of disadvantage within EPAs will have implications for the extent and type of pre-school education required. It would perhaps be advisable for local authorities to cast-out the global term 'disadvantage' and the general designation of 'EPAs' in preference for more detailed and specific characterizations of children and their families. For example, in areas where there is a stable community the demand for pre-school provision may be much lower than in the rapidly shifting population of inner city redevelopment areas where any 'extended-family' network of care for young children may well have broken down. Additionally, the concept of disadvantage has in the main been used to characterize the shifting population of inner city areas without sufficient attention to other groups or areas of the country which may have an equally powerful, if different claim to make for pre-school services. In particular the requirements of pre-school children in rural areas have received less attention. A more useful model for planning than the global EPA concept is to make a detailed assessment of the various requirements of different sections of the population, rather than just the groups who have traditionally been labelled 'disadvantaged'.

An example of one way in which an authority might build on existing provision to develop a service which is appropriate to the character of the area comes from an article by Mollie Clarke (1974). She argues that the large numbers of playgroups may have a special role to play in rural areas. The type of establishments envisaged by the White Paper are unlikely to be suitable to sparsely populated areas where attendance at a nursery class would involve a major bussing operation, undesirable for very young children. An alternative is to use small playgroups as satellites of a central maintained nursery class, guided and assisted by the teachers in that class. Such a scheme would offer a nursery experience for a large group who, though not suffering the obvious disadvantages of inner city children, nevertheless would benefit greatly from a stimulating social experience, to reduce their isolation and broaden their horizons. This is just one example of a model of nursery provision based on local determination of the character and needs of an area; each area is likely to have its own individual requirements.

Factors affecting the take-up of places in nursery provision
(i) *School admission policies*

So far the discussion has dealt with general issues facing a local authority seeking to ensure that pre-school provision is available and appropriate to the children who need it. It is now necessary to examine some particular circumstances affecting children's use of pre-school places. The pattern of uptake is not just determined by existence of nursery establishments and playgroups. The establishments themselves play a role in determining the pattern according to the admission policies they adopt. An effective policy of positive discrimination requires more than providing nursery places in disadvantaged areas, it must also ensure that they are used by the disadvantaged children in that area.

The selection of which children will receive a place in the nursery is one of the more difficult tasks which any head may be required to perform. Most nursery establishments have a long waiting list. The head must decide which of these children should be offered a full-time place and which a part-time place. Inevitably some cannot be offered a place at all. This decision is particularly critical at a time when demand far exceeds the supply of places. The amount of guidance given to heads differs between local authorities. Some local authorities provide a list of home background characteristics which indicate that a child may be in special need of the experience of nursery education, e.g. one-parent family, poor home circumstances. Also in some authorities, a small number of places are reserved for children in special need who may have been referred by social workers, medical practitioners, etc. But it is usually the head teacher who must ultimately make the decisions which will determine the composition of the nursery and the number of disadvantaged children who are able to benefit from the experience. None of the research reported to date has examined in detail policy and practice with regard to selective admission. But it seems likely that active selection is occurring much less frequently than would be required to ensure places for all the most disadvantaged children. Instead, faced with the possibility of irate parents declaring that 'so and so' had jumped the queue heads may prefer to adopt the apparently 'fair' procedure of taking children according to age or position on the waiting list. In theory, this should make it equally likely for children from different social backgrounds to obtain a place. But in practice we may suspect that the children who obtain the places will be those whose parents have most eagerly placed their child's name on the waiting list at the earliest possible opportunity; and these are likely to be the more advantaged groups. To implement a true policy of allocating places based on 'need' rather than 'demand' requires much more active selection of children for the few nursery places available.

(ii) *The attitude of parents*

But there are other good reasons why children who might most benefit from experience of nursery education may not obtain a place, reasons which are outside the direct control of the school. Parents may not endeavour to obtain a place. Willem van der Eyken and Sheila Shinman have conducted a study which has isolated some of these groups of mothers.

The area chosen for study was a council housing estate occupied predominantly by families from social classes IV and V, semi- and unskilled manual workers. This district was not considered to suffer high social stress and only a small proportion of the mothers were in employment; consequently the two factors which are traditionally associated with the desirability of nursery attendance were not operating in this situation.

The first stage of the survey was conducted before there was any kind of pre-school provision on the estate. This identified three groups of mothers according to their use of provision and attitude to it:

Group I: Not using provision and not wishing to.
Group II: Not using any provision but would like to do so.
Group III: Already using some kind of provision outside the area.

The second stage of the survey followed after a council-sponsored playgroup had been established in the district within easy walking distance of all the homes. All mothers were informed of the existence of the playgroup and told that a place for their child was guaranteed. The study monitored mothers' subsequent use of the provision. The results of this second stage suggested to the researchers that a threefold division was an over-simplification. It had not adequately captured more subtle but perhaps more significant influences governing take-up of pre-school places. These influences were related to the mother's motivation and attitude to her child. The critical sub division, between mothers with a 'positive' or 'negative' attitude, turned out to be equally applicable to all three groups.

Thus, Group II who had said they would like their child to attend pre-school provision were divided between those whose children were subsequently regular attenders, and those whose children failed to attend after the first few weeks. Although Group I mothers had stated that they would not seek a place for their child, the group seemed to be divided between those who believed that the right place for their child was at home and those who 'couldn't be bothered' or 'didn't see the need'. Similarly, Group III mothers were divided between those whose children were already attending some form of provision because of their own determination and effort (e.g. in the case of the few working mothers) and those who had been referred by social workers etc., as in special need. In short there appears to be a common factor associated with the variations in the three groups. The 'passive', 'reluctant' and 'apathetic' mothers in each of the three groups were united on numerous aspects of social background and experiences.

The circumstances of families in this district were of a particular kind, and the pre-school provision being offered was in the form of a playgroup. No doubt similar studies conducted in different localities in relation to other types of provision would generate other patterns of association between family circumstances, parental attitude, and use of pre-school services. Nevertheless as a model of the type of complex influences which determine whether a child attends pre-school provision the research is very valuable. It suggests that any assessment of the need for pre-school provision must not simply take into account whether parents say they would like a place for their child, nor whether they actually take up a place when one is available. Much more account must be taken of the motives of parents and their attitudes to their children. (Further details of the design and results of the study may be found in Shinman, 1975).

What methods could be adopted to ensure that these children obtain a place in pre-school provision, even though their parents may not actively seek one? If nursery education is to reach the children who *need* it as well as those whose parents *want* it a much more active effort must be made to locate the families of these children and ensure they take up a place. Local authorities were offered some guidance on this by the Circular 2/73:

'It is important that children from economically and culturally deprived homes should not be put at a further disadvantage because their parents are uninformed about nursery education or diffident about taking the steps necessary to secure a place in a nursery unit. It may be desirable to take positive steps to publicize the expansion of provision in areas of social disadvantage so as to encourage parents whose children are most in need of nursery education to apply for the places available.'

(DES, 1973)

Experiments with home visitors and educational social workers have been described in the previous chapter. But while waiting lists for places in existing nurseries are embarrassingly long and continue to grow, it is not surprising that authorities and heads are reluctant to go out of their way to generate new demand. Nevertheless, the importance of extending the referral system, increasing co—operation between school and social workers and health visitors and actively seeking out the children who would most benefit from nursery experience must be borne in mind in planning any further expansion.

(iii) *The circumstances of families*

Some groups of children do not receive nursery education experience because their parents lack the initiative to seek it for their children. Another important group are those who are excluded because current pre-school provision is inappropriate to the circumstances of their families, in particular those whose mothers work.

A recent report of the Department of Employment (1974) provides evidence of the growing number of married women who for various reasons are seeking employment. The percentage of married women at work has doubled every 20 years since 1931, when 10 per cent were in employment, to 22 per cent in 1951 and 42 per cent in 1971. The report uses data from the General Household Survey to show that the care and education of their young children is an important influence on whether mothers take up employment (Department of Employment, 1974, p.14). Thirty-nine per cent of all the women who were intending to work at some time but were unable to do so because of the need to look after their children, would have brought forward their plans to return to work if satisfactory arrangements could have been made to look after their children. Of course women with young children are amongst the smallest group within these figures, but their numbers are also on the increase; 18.8 per cent of women with children under five and 38.5 per cent of women with children five- to-ten-years-old were in employment in 1971, according to figures presented in 'Social Trends' (OPCS, 1973b).

Unfortunately a lot of mothers are not in a position to wait until satisfactory arrangements are available for the care of their children before returning to work. These mothers must work out of financial necessity, particularly if they are one of the 240,000 single parents with children under five-years-old whose plight has been described in the Finer Report (DHSS, 1974b). These mothers are struggling to bring up families on their own often in the inner city areas where the cost of living is at its highest.

These parents have traditionally made use of the day nurseries which are now provided by the social services departments, but the numbers of these in England and Wales declined rapidly after the war, from 903 in 1949 to 486 in 1959 and 444 in 1969 (DHSS, 1974a). Increasingly they are inadequate to cope with the demand. Parents have turned to the only alternative — child-minders.

Brian Jackson has graphically described the potential dangers to children who have been left with illegal child-minders.

'In our blue folders lies a note: "There were seven small children in one room ranged along a table, being fed from the same bowl with the same spoon. Each pair of enormous eyes followed the spoon hungrily. It was like a scene from Dickens. My most unacceptable experiences were finding rows of pink and royal blue carrycots (in each a baby) parked like packaged battery chickens in a garage and for this the mothers paid £3. a week. Was it evil, ignorance or desperation that made a young mother in the centre of one of the world's ten richest countries do that? What made eleven of them do it? Now, several years the wiser, I can ask what makes up to 100,000 poor mothers seek illegal day care for their child?

(Brian Jackson, 1973, p. 522)

Brian Jackson has since revised his estimate of the numbers of unregistered childminders to 330,000 (*Guardian*, 24th July, 1974). What is particularly worrying is the prevalence of these so-called 'illegal' child-minders who are not registered with social services departments and therefore receive no supervision and advice. Brian Jackson's Child Minding Research Unit is endeavouring to monitor the situation and co-ordinate support for the child-minders. In their latest Action-Register (Jackson, 1974) it is estimated that in several Manchester districts surveyed the ratio of illegal to legal child minders is in excess of 11 to one.

An impressive number of voluntary groups as well as local authorities are now organizing schemes for child-minders including courses, teacher-visitors and toy lending schemes. One way of upgrading the quality of experience of child-minded children is by encouraging child-minders to bring children to the nursery part-time. Contact with the schools can also have a positive influence on child—minders' understanding of the educational needs of their children. Amongst the most promising ventures we may single out a radio-amnesty for child-minders (Jackson and Knight, 1975); salaries paid to child-minders by local authorities; and production of a low cost toy kit by a commercial manufacturer.

The growth of child minding illustrates one response to inadequate and inappropriate nursery provision; the development of industrial creches or nurseries is another. Enterprising industrial concerns have used free or low cost care for young children as an incentive to mothers to work in the factory. A report on 22 of these has recently been prepared by the Institute of Personnel Management (Day, 1975), and includes a section for managers of industry on 'How to set up a Nursery'. Like child-minders, these nurseries are catering for those children who may be 'at risk'. As such they need to be guided and supervised, and particularly the educational content of the programmes improved.

What role can maintained provision play in the care and education of children whose mothers work? Both day nurseries and nursery education establishments may be criticized for failing to cater for the needs of these children.

In day nurseries the emphasis is on care, which can be provided for children whose mothers work a full day. But the lack of a major educational element in the programme of the day nursery may serve to increase the disadvantage of children compared with those who attend the more educationally-orientated nursery school or class. And, not unimportantly, the families must usually pay for use of the day nursery; by comparison, the child-minders are cheaper. (A full account of day care facilities in Britain is provided in Kellmer Pringle and Naidhoo, 1975.)

A complementary criticism may be levelled at the nursery school and class. Although providing an educational programme, the hours of attendance of the nursery do not match with the requirements of most types of employment. Even full-time attendance, which is available to only a few, is not likely to suit many working mothers, lasting as it does from 9 am to 3.30 pm, unless they can arrange for someone to take the child to school in the morning and collect him in the evening. And, of course, educational provision is free. As a consequence of these different functions and aims of the establishments, many of the children who might most need an educational experience are denied it. This style of social and educational planning does little to commend our success in implementing the much coveted philosophy of equality of educational opportunity. Many of the problems arise because provision is the responsibility of two local government departments.

Recognizing this anomaly, Plowden had recommended setting up nursery units which included education and care (Central Advisory Council for Education, 1967, vol. I para. 313—315), but this was not included in the White Paper and Circular 2/73 which did not propose any modification to the traditional pattern and allowed for only 15 per cent of three- and four-year-olds to attend full-time. Nevertheless, a few centres have been set up as a result of co-operation and joint planning between social services and education departments. The centres vary considerably in the extent to which integration is achieved between the day nursery and nursery school elements of the establishment. Descriptions of the work of two of these centres may be found in Midwinter (1974) and Brennan (1974). Another example of integrating care and education is provided by a voluntary centre set up by the Thomas Coram Foundation, which has managed to avoid many of the problems which are associated with co-operative planning between two departments of local government. A research project at the National Children's Bureau is at present evaluating some of these centres. (For further discussion see Tizard J., 1975; for a discussion of similar issues in the American context see Blackstone, 1973).

There is also an alternative strategy which reconciles the problem of providing education and care at least for three- and four-year-olds, but works within an existing educational establishment. A pilot scheme to provide an 'extended-day' within a nursery school has been described by Eileen Totten (1975).

There are two particular features of the scheme, which is supported by a special grant from the local education authority. The first is the flexibility in the hours children attend, arranged to meet the needs of children and their families. The nursery school is open 49 weeks of the year from 8 am to 6 pm. Two-thirds of the children on roll are part-timers, the remaining third attend full-time. Extended hours are available to both full-and part-timers, and approximately one-quarter of the roll benefit from the scheme in various ways. Much of the concern which is expressed about providing day-long care may arise because of fears for the consequences of mother and child being separated for long hours. This fear may be unwarranted. Parents are discouraged from leaving their children for the whole school day but in practice very few seek to do so. Most children attend for an extended part-time day, a few come early in the morning and stay until after lunch, but the greatest demand is for children to come in the afternoon and stay on after normal school hours. Either of these arrangements enables the mother to do a part-time job, and these extended part-time hours are likely to meet employers' demands better than the traditional hours.

The appropriateness of arranging *extended part-time* education for these children is supported by evidence from the 1971 census. *Social Trends* (OPCS, 1973b) shows that the 18.8 per cent of women with children under five who are in employment, comprises only 5.7 per cent who work over 30 hours per week; most, 12.1 per cent, work under 30 hours per week. In keeping with the flexibility of the scheme some children attend normal (full-time or part-time) hours during term-time but also attend during the holidays. The scheme also allows for emergency situations (e.g. family illness) when the child may attend for the extended day on a short-term basis. Staffing has been adapted to make this flexibility possible. Extra staff have been recruited to work different hours from usual. There is a morning and an afternoon shift with a big overlap during the time when most of the children are at the nursery.

The second feature of the scheme is that the school does not seek to substitute for the day nursery by providing day care; rather the school attempts to provide 'extended *education*'. There is a teacher present at all times supervising activities. The 'extended day' children are fully integrated within the normal nursery groups, and continue to use the nursery equipment out of school hours. This emphasis on extended education is a departure even from the efforts of combined nursery school/day care centres to ensure that children needing day care are not deprived of an educational experience. The experiment takes the argument one step further. The children do not only need the normal 'allowance' of nursery education experience, which is often only a very small part of their waking life; they need a continuous educational experience if they are to start school having had the same basic experiences as other children.

There are some additional advantages in this approach over the nursery school/day centres, which are often very costly to purpose-build, whereas this approach is simply making use of the normal facilities of a good nursery school. Although the extended day increases the running costs, especially because extra teachers must be employed, this school is making more efficient use of resources and staff than the normal school (or class) and could provide the near-equivalent of a full-time place (a five-hour morning or a five-hour afternoon) for a much larger number of children than would be possible in a nursery of similar size but operating traditional hours.

This scheme is only an experiment but presents promising possibilities for ensuring the attendance of three- to five-year-old children who might not otherwise gain a place. Of course any scheme which recognizes a responsibility of the school to provide an education for children out of normal school hours inevitably leads to the question of what happens to the children when they enter the primary school. Being a latch-key child at five may potentially be as harmful as being child-minded at three.

Conclusions

A number of conclusions can be drawn from these issues. Firstly, there can be no uniform pattern of nursery provision. Families live in different circumstances which affect the type of nursery provision they are able to use. This must be taken into account when planning for the education of their children. The model of part-time attendance may be suitable for those families where only one parent works, and the principle role of the other is to care for the children. But increasingly both parents are finding it economically necessary to work at least part-time even while their children are quite young. Secondly if the policy of making nursery education available for disadvantaged children is to be put into practice then expansion must not simply involve passively making places available for those who seek it; it must involve actively seeking out those who need it. This will require more active co-ordination of the school with services which are able to reach into the homes of children and identify those in need.

Any of these ambitious schemes depend, of course, on the financial resources of local authorities, and their willingness to use them to develop their services for young children. Since the 1972 White Paper, there has been a great surge of optimism, that at last adequate educational provision would be made available for the under-fives. It is to be hoped that the slow start to the expansion programme which we are currently witnessing reflects the depressing economic climate and not a failure to recognize the crucial importance to young children and their families that adequate facilities for education and care are made available.

REFERENCES

ACLAND, H. (1971). 'What is a "bad" school?', *New Society*. 9 Sept.

BARKER-LUNN, J.C. (1970). *Streaming in the Primary School*. Slough: NFER.

BARNES, J. (1975). *Educational Priority Volume 3: Curriculum Innovation in London's EPAs*. London: HMSO.

BARNEY, D. (1975). *Who Gets to Pre-School? The Availability of Pre-School Provision in New Zealand*. Wellington: New Zealand Council for Educational Research.

BEREITER, C. and ENGLEMANN, S. (1966). *Teaching Disadvantaged Children in the Preschool*. Englewood Cliffs, New Jersey: Prentice-Hall.

BERNSTEIN, B. (1970). 'Education cannot compensate for Society', *New Society*, 26 Feb.

BERNSTEIN, B. (1971a). 'A sociolinguistic approach to socialisation: with some reference to educability'. In: HYMES, D. and GUMPERZ, J.J. (Eds) *Directions in Socio-linguistics*. New York: Holt, Rinehart & Winston.

BERNSTEIN, B. (1971b). *Class, Codes and Control Volume 1: Theoretical Studies towards a sociology of Language*. London: Routledge & Kegan Paul.

BERNSTEIN, B. (1973). *Class, Codes and Control Volume 2: Applied Studies towards a Sociology of Language*. London: Routledge & Kegan Paul.

BISSELL, J.S. (1973). 'Planned variation in Head Start and Follow Through'. In: STANLEY, J.C. (Ed) *Compensatory Education for Children. Ages 2 to 8*. London: The Johns Hopkins University Press.

BLACKSTONE, T. (1971). *A Fair Start: The Provision of Pre-School Education*. London: Allen Lane, The Penguin Press.

BLACKSTONE, T. (1973). *Education and day care for young children in need: the American experience*. London: Bedford Square Press.

BLANK, M. (1973). *Teaching Disadvantaged Children in the Pre-School: A Dialogue Approach*. Columbus, Ohio: Merrill.

BLANK, M. and SOLOMON, F. (1969). 'How shall the disadvantaged child be taught?', *Child Development*. 40, 1, 47–61.

BLOOM, B.S. (1964). *Stability and Change in Human Characteristics*. New York: Wiley.

BOEHM, A.E. (1969). *Boehm Test of Basic Concepts*. New York: The Psychological Corporation.

BOYDELL, D. (1975a). 'Individual attention: "the child's eye view"', *Education 3—13*, 3, 1.

BOYDELL, D. (1975b). 'Systematic observation in the informal classroom'. In: CHANAN, G. and DELAMONT, S. (Eds) *Frontiers of classroom research*. Slough: NFER.

BRENNAN, P. (1974). 'Glossop centre goes all-out for integration', Supplement to *Education*, 22 Nov.

BRIMER, M.A. and DUNN, L.M. (1962). *English Picture Vocabulary Test, pre-school and Test I*. Bristol: Educational Evaluation Enterprises.

BRONFENBRENNER, U. (1973). *Is Early Education Effective?* Cornell University Press.

BROPHY, J.E. and GOOD, T.L. (1970). 'Teachers' communication of differential expectations for children's classroom performance', *Journal of Educational Psychology*, **61, 5, 365—74.**

BRUNER, J.S., OLVER, R.R., GREENFIELD, P.M. *et al.* (1966). *Studies in Cognitive Growth*. New York: Wiley.

CAMPBELL, P.T., and ERLEBACHER, A. (1970). 'How regression artefacts in quasi-experimental evaluations can mistakenly make compensatory education look harmful'. In: HELLMUTH, J. (Ed) *The Disadvantaged Child Vol III*. New York: Brunner/Mazel.

CAZDEN, C.B. (1965). Environmental assistance to the child's acquisition of grammar. Unpublished doctoral dissertation, Harvard Unversity. Reported in: CAZDEN, C.B. (1972). *Child Language and Education*. London: Holt, Rinehart and Winston.

CAZDEN, C.B. (forthcoming). 'Concentrated and contrived encounters: suggestions for language assessment in early childhood education'. In: DAVIES, A. (Ed) *Language and Learning in Early Childhood*. London: Heinemann.

CAZDEN, C.B., JOHN, V.P. and HYMES, D. *Functions of Language in the Classroom*. London: Teachers College Press.

CENTRAL ADVISORY COUNCIL FOR EDUCATION (ENGLAND) (1967a). *Children and their Primary Schools: Vol I. The Report*. (The Plowden Report). London: HMSO.

CENTRAL ADVISORY COUNCIL FOR EDUCATION (ENGLAND) (1967b). *Children and their Primary Schools: Vol II. Research and Surveys*. (The Plowden Report). London: HMSO.

CENTRAL STATISTICAL OFFICE (1974). *Annual Abstract of Statistics No. III* London: HMSO.

CHAZAN, M. (Ed) (1973). *Compensatory Education*. London: Butterworth.

CHAZAN, M. (forthcoming). *Studies of Infant School Children. Vols I. II. III*. London: Basil Blackwell.

CHAZAN, M., LAING, A. and JACKSON, S. (1971). *Just Before*

School. Oxford: Basil Blackwell.

CHOMSKY, N. (1965). *Aspects of the Theory of Syntax*. Cambridge, Mass.: M.I.T. Press.

CICIRELLI, V.G., GRANGER, R.L. *et al*. (1969). *The Impact of Headstart: an Evaluation of the Effects of Headstart on Children's Cognitive and Affective Development. Vol I*. Washington D.C.: Westinghouse Learning Corporation and Ohio University.

CLARKE, M. (1974). 'Being truly rural, minus resources, is no idyll', Supplement to *Education*, 22 Nov.

COUNCIL OF EUROPE (1974). *Compensatory Education* (Report of Strasbourg workshop). Strasbourg: Documentation Centre for Education in Europe.

COUNCIL OF EUROPE (1975). *Problems in the evaluation of pre-school education*. Strasbourg: Documentation Centre for Education in Europe.

DAY, C. (1975). *Company Day Nurseries*. London: Institute of Personnel Management.

DAVIE, R., BUTLER, N. and GOLDSTEIN, H. (1972). *From Birth to Seven*. London: Longmans.

DEPARTMENT OF EDUCATION AND SCIENCE (DES) (1972). *White Paper, Education: A Framework for Expansion*. Cmnd 5174. London: HMSO.

DEPARTMENT OF EDUCATION AND SCIENCE (DES) (1973). *Nursery Education*. DES Circular 2/73.

DEPARTMENT OF EDUCATION AND SCIENCE (DES) (1974). *Statistics of Education 1974. Schools Vol I*. London: HMSO.

DEPARTMENT OF EDUCATION AND SCIENCE (DES) (1975a). *Pre-School Education and Care*: some topics requiring research and development projects. DES: unpublished.

DEPARTMENT OF EDUCATION AND SCIENCE (DES) (1975b). *A Language for Life*. London: HMSO.

DEPARTMENT OF EDUCATION AND SCIENCE (DES) (1975c). *Local Authority Expenditure in 1976/77 — Forward Planning*. DES Circular 10/75.

DEPARTMENT OF EMPLOYMENT (1974). *Women and Work: A Statistical Survey*. D. of E. Manpower Paper No. 9. London: HMSO.

DEPARTMENT OF HEALTH AND SOCIAL SECURITY (DHSS) (1974a). *Health and Personal Social Services Statistics for England*. London: HMSO.

DEPARTMENT OF HEALTH AND SOCIAL SECURITY (DHSS) (1974b). *Report of the Committee on One-Parent Families*. London: HMSO.

DOUGLAS, J.W.B. (1964). *The Home and the School*. London: Macgibbon & Kee.

DUNN, L.M., HORTON, K.B. and SMITH, J.O. (1968). *Peabody Language Development Kit, Level P.* Minnesota: American Guidance Service Inc.

EDUCATION (1975). 'Nursery Schools Now'. Supplement to *Education*, 28 Nov.

EDUCATIONAL TESTING SERVICE (ETS) (1966). *Cooperative Primary Maths Test.*

EISENBERG, L. *et al.* (1962). 'Use of teacher ratings in a mental health study: a method for measuring the effectiveness of a therapeutic nursery program', *American Journal of Public Health*, **52**, 1, 18—28.

EYSENCK, H.J. (1971). *Race. Intelligence and Education.* London: Temple Smith.

FERGUSON, N. *et al.* (1971). 'The Plowden Report's recommendations for identifying children in need of extra help', *Educational Research*, **13**, 3.

GAHAGAN, D.M. and GAHAGAN, G.A. (1970). *Talk Reform.* London: Routledge and Kegan Paul.

GARDNER, D.E.M. (1956). *The Education of Young Children.* London: Methuen.

GARNER, J. and BING, M. (1973). 'Inequalities of teacher-pupil contacts', *British Journal of Educational Psychology*, **32**, 3.

GRAY, S. and KLAUS, R. (1965). 'An experimental pre-school program for culturally-deprived children', *Child Development*, **36**, 4.

GATES—MACGINITIE. (1972). *Reading Test Primary A.* New York: Columbia University, Teachers College Press. Distributed by NFER.

GREENE, J. (1972). *Psycholinguistics: Chomsky and Psychology.* Harmondsworth: Penguin.

HADOW REPORT (1933). *Report of the Consultative Committee on Infant and Nursery Education.* London: HMSO.

HALLIDAY, M.A.K. (1973). 'On the functional basis of language'. In: BERNSTEIN, B. (Ed) *Class, Codes, and Control Volume 2.* London: Routledge and Kegan Paul.

HALLIDAY M.A.K. (1975). *Learning how to Mean: explorations in the development of language.* London: Edward Arnold.

HALSEY, A.H. (Ed) (1972). *Educational Priority Volume 1: EPA Problems and Policies.* London: HMSO.

HERTZIG, M.E., BIRCH, M.G. *et al.* (1968). 'Class and ethnic differences in the responsiveness of pre-school children to cognitive demands', *Monograph of the Society for Research in Child Development.* **33**, 1.

HERZOG, E., NEWCOMB, C.H. and CISIN, I.M. (1972). 'Double deprivation: the less they have the less they learn'. In: RYAN, S. (Ed) A report on longitudinal evaluations of pre-school programs. Washington D.C.: Office of Child Development.

HESS, R.D. (1966). *Techniques for assessing cognitive and social abilities of children and parents in Headstart*. Princeton, New Jersey: Educational Testing Service.

HESS, R. and SHIPMAN, V. (1965). 'Early experience and the socialization of cognitive modes in children', *Child Dev.*, **36**, 3.

HONEY, M., NEALE, A. and THOMPSON, Q. (1973. 'Day care and play for under-fives in Greenwich', *Quarterly Bulletin of the Intelligence Unit*, **23**, June. Greater London Council

HOWE. M.J.A. (1975) 'Pygmalion and after: new research into the effects of teacher's expectations on school children', *Education 3—13*, **3**, 1.

HUNT. J.McV. (1969). 'Has compensatory education failed? Has it been attempted?. In: *Environment, Heredity, and Intelligence*. Harvard Educational Review Reprint Series No. 2.

ISAACS, S. (1968). *The Nursery Years*. New York: Schocken Books.

JACKSON, B. (1973) 'The Child Minders', *New Society*, 29 Nov.

JACKSON, B. (1974). *Child Minding. Action Register Number Two*. National Educational Research and Development Trust.

JACKSON, B. and KNIGHT, B. (1975). *The Nottingham Experiment*. The National Educational Research and Development Trust.

JENCKS, C. *et al.* (1973). *Inequality: Reassessment of the Effect of Family and Schooling in America*. London: Allen Lane.

JENSEN, A.R. (1969). 'How much can we boost IQ and scholastic achievement?', *Havard Educational Review*. **39**, 1.

KARNES, M.B. (1968). *Final report: research and development program on preschool disadvantaged children*. Urbana, Illinois: Institute for Research of Exceptional Children.

KARNES, M.B. (1973). 'Evaluation and implications of research with young handicapped and low-income children'. In: STANLEY, J.C. (Ed) *Compensatory Education for Children. Ages 2 to 8*. London: The Johns Hopkins University Press.

KAY, J.L. (1975). 'The direction of the Nursery Education Research Programme', *Trends in Education*, **3**, 22—8.

KELLMER PRINGLE, M. and NADHOO, S. (1975). *Early child care in Britain*. London: Gordon and Breach.

KIRK, S.A., McCARTHY, J.J. and KIRK, W.D. (1968). *Illinois Test of Psycholinguistic Abilities*. London: University of illinois Press.

LABOV, W. (1969). 'The logic of nonstandard English', *Georgetown Monographs on language and linguistics*, **22**.

LAWRENCE, E. (Ed) (1952). *Friedrich Froebel and English Education*. University of London Press.

LAWTON, D. (1963). 'Social class differences in language development: a study of some samples of written work', *Language and Speech*, **6**, 120.

LAWTON, D. (1968). *Social Class and Education*. London: Routledge & Kegan Paul.

LILLEY, I.M. (1967). *Friedrich Froebel. A Selection from his writings*. Cambridge: Cambridge University Press.

LITTLE, A. and SMITH, G. (1971). *Strategies of Compensation: A Review of Educational Projects for the Disadvantaged in the United States*. Centre for Educational Research and Innovation (CERI), Organisation for Economic Co-operation and Development.

LOZELLS SOCIAL DEVELOPMENT CENTRE (1975). *Wednesday's Children: A report on under-fives provision in Handsworth*. London: Community Relations Commission.

LURIA, A.R. (1961). *The Role of Speech in the Regulation of Normal and Abnormal Behaviour*. New York: Pergamon Press.

McMILLAN, N. (1930). *The Nursery School*. New York: E.P. Dutton & Co. Inc.

MEDLEY, D.M., SCHLUCK, C. and AMES, N. (1968). *A manual for PROSE recorders*. Princeton, New Jersey: Educational Testing Service.

MIDWINTER, E. (1972). *Priority Education. an Account of the Liverpool Project*. Harmondsworth: Penguin.

MIDWINTER, E. (1974). *Preschool Priorities*. London: Ward Lock Educational.

MOFFETT, J. (1968). *Teaching the Universe of Discourse*. Boston, Mass.: Houghton Mifflin.

MORRISON, C.M., WATT, J.S. and LEE, T.R. (Eds) (1974). *Educational Priority Volume 5: EPA—A Scottish Study*. Edinburgh: HMSO.

OFFICE OF POPULATION, CENSUSES AND SURVEYS (OPCS) (1973a). *The General Household Survey*. London: HMSO.

OFFICE OF POPULATION CENSUSES AND SURVEYS (OPCS) (1973b). *Social Trends Volume 4*. Central Statistical Office OPCS. London: HMSO.

OSBORN, A.F. (1975). *The Demand for Pre-School Provision*. Unpublished paper presented to Somerset PPA.

OSGOOD, C.E. (1957). 'Motivational dynamics of language behaviour'. In: *Nebraska Symposium on Motivation*. Lincoln Nebraska: University of Nebraska Press.

PARRY, M. and ARCHER, H. (1974). *Preschool Education*. School Council Research Studies. London: MacMillan Education Ltd.,

PARRY, M. and ARCHER, H. (1975). *Two to Five, a Handbook for Students and Teachers*. London: MacMillan Education Ltd.

PAYNE, J. (1974). *Educational Priority Volume 2: E.P.A. Surveys and Statistics*. London: HMSO.

POULTON, G.A. and JAMES, T. (1975). *Pre-School learning in the*

Community. Strategies for change. London: Routledge & Kegan Paul.
PRE-SCHOOL PLAYGROUPS ASSOCIATION (PPA) (1974). *A quarter of a million Pre-School Children.* London: PPA.
QUIGLEY, H. (1971). 'Nursery teachers' reactions to the Peabody Language Development Kit', *Br.J.educ. Psychol.* **41**, 155—62.
QUIGLEY, H. and HUDSON, M. (1974). *British Manual to the Peabody Language Development Kit (Level P).* Windsor: Test Division, NFER Publishing Co. Ltd.
RADIN, N. (1972). 'Three degrees of parental involvement in a pre-school program: impact on mothers and children', *Child Development*, **43**, 1355—64.
RESNICK, L.B. (1972). 'Teacher behaviour in the informal classroom', *Journal of Curriculum Studies.* **4**.
REYNELL, J. (1969). *Reynell Developmental Language Scales.* Windsor: NFER Publishing Company.
ROSENTHAL, R. and JACOBSON, L. (1968). *Pygmalion in the classroom: Teacher expectation and pupils' intellectual development.* New York: Holt, Rinehart & Winston.
RUTTER, M. (1967). 'The Children's Behaviour questionnaire for completion by teachers: preliminary findings,' *Journal of Child Psychology and Psychiatry* **8**, 1—11.
SHARROCK, A.N. (1970). *Home School Relations: their importance in Education.* London: MacMillan
SHINMAN, S. (1975). *Parental Response to Pre—School Provision.* Brunel University Department of Education.
SINCLAIR-DE-ZWART, H. (1969). 'Developmental psycholinguistics'. In: ELKIND, D. and FLAVEL, J. (Eds) *Studies in Cognitive Development.* Oxford University Press.
SJOLUND, A. (1973). *Day Care Institutions and Children's Development.* Farnborough: Saxon Books.
SLOBIN, D.T. (1971). *Psycholinguistics.* Glenview, Illinois: Scott, Foresman and Company.
SMILANSKY, S. (1968). *The Effects of Sociodramatic Play on Disadvantaged Pre-School Children.* New York: Wiley.
SMITH, G. (1975). *Educational Priority Volume 4: The West Riding EPA.* London: HMSO.
SMITH, G. and JAMES, T. (1975). 'The effects of preschool education: some American and British evidence', *Oxford Review of Education.* **1**, 3, 221—38.
STANLEY, J.C. (1972). *Preschool Programs for the Disadvantaged.* London: The Johns Hopkins University Press.
STANLEY, J.C. (1973). *Compensatory Education for Children ages Two to Eight: Recent Studies of Educational Intervention.* London: The Johns Hopkins University Press.

STOTT, D.H., WILLIAMS, H.L. and SHARP, J.D. (1976). 'Effective-ness — motivation in pre-school children', *Educational Research*, **18**, 2.

SWIFT, J.W. (1964). 'Effects of early group experience: the nursery school and day nursery'. In: HOFFMAN, M.L. and HOFF-MAN, L.W. (Eds) *Review of Child Development Research*. New York: Russell Sage Foundation.

TAYLOR, P.H., EXON, G., and HOLLEY, B. (1972). *A study of Nursery Education*. Schools Council Working Paper 41. London: Evans/Methuen.

THOMAS, V. (1973). 'Children's use of language in the nursery', *Educational Research*, **15**, 3.

THOMPSON, B. (1975). 'Adjustment to school', *Educational Research*. **17**, 2.

TIZARD, B. (1975). *Pre-School Education in Great Britain. A Report to SSRC*. Slough: NFER.

TIZARD, B., COOPERMAN, O. *et al.* (1972). 'Environmental effects on language development: a study of young children in longstay residential nurseries', *Child Development*, **43**, 337–58.

TIZARD, B., PHILPS, J. and PLEWIS, I. (in press). 'Staff behaviour in pre-school centres', *Journal of Child Psychology and Psychiatry*.

TIZARD. J. (1975). 'The objectives and organisation of educational and day care services for young children', *Oxford Review of Education*, **1**, 3.

TOTTEN, E. (1975). 'Extended day nursery', *Times Educational Supplement*, 14th Feb.

TOUGH, Y.J. (1973a). 'Communication skills in Early Childhood Project', *Dialogue*, **14**, Summer.

TOUGH, Y.J. (1973b). *Focus on Meaning: Talking to Some Purpose with Young children*. London: George Allen & Unwin.

TOUGH, Y.J. (1973c). 'The language of young children'. In: CHAZAN, M. (Ed) *Education in the Early Years*. University of Swansea Press.

TOUGH, Y.J. (1975). 'Language in open education', *Education 3–13*, **3**, 1.

TOUGH', Y.J. (forthcoming a). 'Children and programmes: how shall we educate the young child?'. In: DAVIES, A. (Ed) *Language and Learning in Early Childhood*. London: Heinemanns.

TOUGH, Y.J. (forthcoming b). *The Development of Meaning*. London: George Allen and Unwin.

VYGOTSKY, L.S. (1962). *Thought and Language*. Cambridge, Mass: MIT Press.

WEBB, L. (1974). *Purpose & Practice in Nursery Education*. Oxford: Basil Blackwell.

WEDGE, P, and PROSSER, H. (1973). *Born to Fail?* London: Arrow Books Ltd.

WEIKART, D.P. (1972). 'Relationship of curriculum teaching and learning in pre-school education'. In: STANLEY, J.C. (Ed) *Pre-School Programs for the Disadvantaged*. London: The Johns Hopkins University Press.

WILLIAMS, F. and NAREMORE, R.C. (1969a). 'Social class differences in children's syntactic performance: a quantitative analysis of field study data', *Journal of Speech and Hearing Research* **12**, 777–93.

WILLIAMS, F. and NAREMORE, R.C. (1969b). 'On the functional analysis of social class differences in modes of speech', *Speech Monographs*, **36**, 77–102.

WILLIAMS, H.L. (1973). 'Compensatory education in the nursery school'. In: CHAZAN, M. *(Ed) Compensatory Education.*

WOODHEAD, M. (Ed) (1976). *An Experiment in Nursery Education*. Slough: NFER.

ZIGLER, E.F. and BUTTERFIELD, E.L. (1968). 'Motivational aspects of change in IQ test performance of culturally deprived nursery school children', *Child Dev.*, **39**, 1–14.